AMERICAN URBAN TYPOLOGIES

KEY WEST FLORIDA

ERICK VALLE

VILLAGE PUBLISHERS

Published in the United States of America in 1995 by

DISTRIBUTED BY

Village Publishers, Inc.
P.O.BOX 832137
Miami, Florida 33283-2137

Senior Editors: Jaime Correa and Estela Valle

Library of Congress Catalog Card Number 95-060111

ISBN 1-886993-00-9 (Soft Cover)

Layout Design By Erick Valle

This book series intends to document domestic architecture within the urban landscape of the Americas. The City of Key West, Florida's historic district was selected in order to reveal the ingredients that make up a memorable place. It presents an alternative choice for the 21st century.

"Towns must not depend on posted signs to identify themselves."

AMERICAN URBAN TYPOLOGIES

Titles forthcoming:

KEY WEST, FLORIDA
CD-ROM .... Mid 1995

NEW ORLEANS, LOUISIANNA
BOOK .... Mid 1995
CD-ROM .... Mid 1995

CHARLESTON, SOUTH CAROLINA
BOOK .... Late 1995
CD-ROM .... Late 1995

SAVANNAH, GEORGIA
BOOK .... Early 1996
CD-ROM .... Early 1996

SAINT AUGUSTINE, FLORIDA
BOOK .... Mid 1996
CD-ROM .... Mid 1996

C O N T E N T S

This publication is dedicated to the individuals who are retaining the ever lasting beauty of the historic district of Key West: "The Conchs"

ACKNOWLEDGEMENTS

My wife's dedication and support has been the foundation upon which I developed this publication; I shall always be grateful for her patience and her intellectual enthusiasm: Estela Valle, architect and town planner. I am also endebted to my parents, parents-in-law and the people who pushed me to make a book out of this research.

My special thanks to the following people and organizations:

University of Miami, School of Architecture

- Roger Schluntz, dean, architect
- Elizabeth Plater-Zyberk, professor, architect and town planner
- Jaime Correa, professor, architect and town planner
- Vincent Scully, professor, historian and critic
- Catherine Lynn, professor and preservationist
- Dr. Branko Kolarevic, professor and director of computing
- Robert Herrick, Bjorn Green, Christopher Jackson, Javier Cordova, Dean Cretsinger and Patricia Shpilberg my talented research assistants

Organizations

- University of Miami
- Key West Planning Department
- Historic Florida Keys Preservation Board
- Library of Congress, Historic Building Surveys Department
- New York Sanborn Map & Publishing Company
- Monroe Public Library in Key West
- South Florida Water Management District
- Autodesk, Inc.
- Environmental Research Systems Institute (ERSI), Inc.

The graphics and layout of this book was done entirely with AutoCad, ArcCad, ArcView, Corel Draw and PageMaker.

CONCH GUEST HOUSE

Towns must not rely on posted signs to identify themselves.

TOWNS FOR THE 21st CENTURY

The intent of this book is to document pertinent urban facts within a traditional American city. It offers a rational approach to the observation of existing places and a choice for building new ones based on these facts. The choice becomes surprisingly clear when particular attention is given to present patterns of development.

In America, the car is still damaging the natural environment. It has spouted the suburban community, the strip shopping center, the regional mall, the office park, the industrial park, etc.; with such degree of freedom and mobilization the American landscape has been subjected to urbanization in its entirety.

America has gone wrong at two scales: at the macro scale (the region) it has lacked development strategies for a cohesive plan aimed at balancing the natural, agricultural and urban systems; at the micro scale (the town) with its standardized codes, it has produced uniformed and standardized environments.

Developers are not diabolic and out to destroy the American landscape. They are simply building what is presently allowed. In this context, taking a critical view and proposing alternatives has become an undeniable emergency.

The new development model includes a wide range of choices and has some of the basic and traditional components found in authentic American cities. This new development model is possible by the introduction of codes that require variation of building types and sizes (available to own, rent, shop, play and work all within walking distances); this alternative choice is grounded on those authentic American town planning principles which have created most of the memorable places where we still search for our beginnings. My challenge has been to understand the principles that govern the type, the urban and architectural codes, and the site conditions.

This publication is not about style, but about a new architectural vocabulary that is by itself traditional and modern. What matters is the code as a guiding help for development. It is my conclusion that memorable places require two elements: first, a detailed master plan that balances the car and the pedestrian and second, the right building type(s). The documentation of building types influencing the morphology of the town is of the essence.

Although this publication focuses only on one city, a forthcoming study will include the domestic architecture of other American towns such as Saint Augustine, Savannah, Charleston and New Orleans. These southeastern towns are some of the most favorite American places and once visited cannot be forgotten.

Building types were selected on the basis of: diversity, affordability and sociability. Buildings which can change over time (Diversity), buildings which use local materials and are of simple construction methods (Affordability), and buildings designed to allow the occupant to participate in daily events that occur on the street (Sociability). In general the building types of Key West allow for a mix of incomes, contribute to the security of the public realm, and are still practical models for new construction .

THE PRESENT URBAN MODEL

> *"Presently, we have but one choice: to work in one zone, to play in another and to school in still another zone. Low density communities seem to appear as large metropolis."*

Codes are based on three principles: safety of the occupants, promotion of health (by creating sanitary restrictions) and easiness of administration; theyneglect, however, to include a vital fourth objective which should guide every development: the coordination of the building and zoning code with the modest dimension of the street section.

It is on streets where visitors interpret the quality of urban life and conceive the desire to come back again. I am convinced that issues of identity are directly influenced by typology. Buildings have a definite responsibility to the common good.

Humans need to see other humans; people watch instinctively; humans also need a place to gather. If such a place existed today in our American neighborhoods, getting to it would be yet another experience, humans need sidewalks. Sadly, communities which integrate human activities are no longer a part of us. The town, the block, the street, the lot, the building, and the landscape need to become once again the ingredients for a viable choice of development.

America seems to be incapable of avoiding the posted-sign phenomena. Words are exploited in an attempt to call attention to a new development: signs with names like Town Center, Village Green, Village Park, etc., and are really parking lots or empty greens. The American dream built in the last 50 years has an identity crisis, but, who are we to blame for the prevailing chaos?

Key West provides a little bit of rationality amidst contemporary chaos. More than a simple documentation effort, this book is about a structural method in which traditional composition elements are dissected to illustrate a beautiful symphony. Just try playing it!

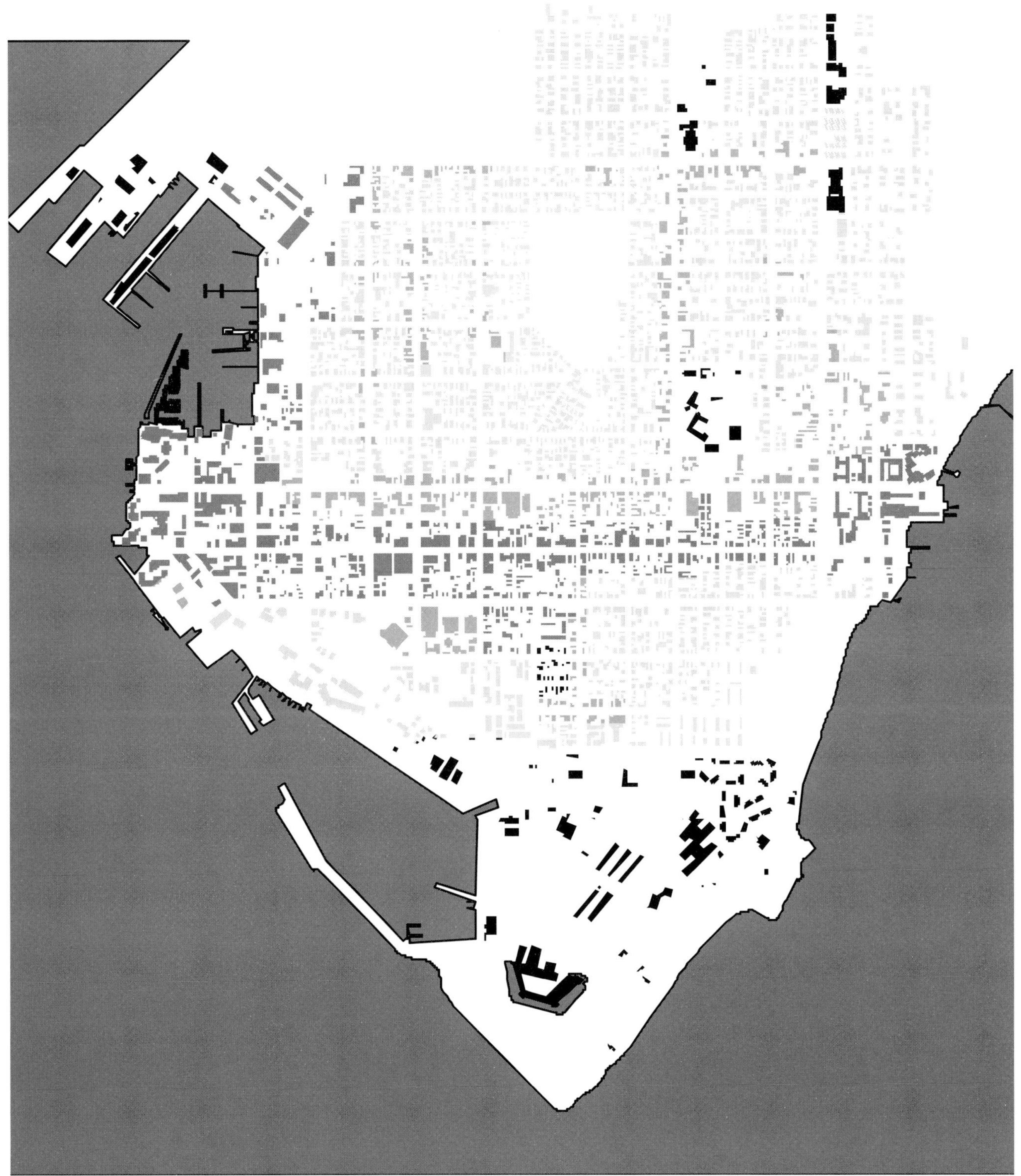

Land Use Map for the historic district of Key West, Florida

BRIEF SUMMARY OF THE URBAN HISTORY

Sketch of History:

- The Florida Keys were occupied by Indians for more than 7,000 years.
- The first credited European contact was Ponce de Leon in 1513. He named the island "Los Martines." Maps identifying the island of Key West existed before that time possibly recorded by either Americo Vespucci or Christopher Columbus.
- Calusa Indians and Ais Indians migrated to Key West before the 18th century.
- In the 1700's the Calusa and Caribe Indians sustained great battles along the beaches leaving a sea of bones and casualties that flooded the beautiful shores. The nickname of "Cayo Hueso" (Bone Island) was assigned to commemorate these bloody events.

Early Permanent Settlement:

- A Spanish gentleman named Juan Pablo Salas acquires "Cayo Hueso" through a Spanish land grant in 1815.
- On December 20, 1821, John W. Simonton bought the Island for $2,000 dollars from Juan Pablo Salas.
- The new owner, John W. Simonton, soon afterwards takes on three additional partners Pardon C. Greene, John Whitehead and John W.C. Fleming.
- The first large arrival of people came from the Bahamas C. 1830.
- The local islanders become known as "Conchs" because of the great abundance of the popular *Queen Conch* shell in the waters of the island.
- Six population booms have characterized the growth: during the 1850's with the ship salvage industry; in the 1860's with cigar factories; in 1912 with the arrival of Flagler's Railroad; in 1938 with the completion of the overseas highway; in 1949 with the shrimp industry; and, since the late 1970's with the arrival of tourism.

N
E
W
S
1995
500 0 500 1000 1500 Feet
KEY WEST, FLORIDA

TOWN GROWTH:

A lesson on flexible growth can be appreciated at the macro scale.

The 1829 map is the earliest recorded platting of Key West. Following the Spanish system of colonial platting, the original owners parceled the blocks into four equal parts. Each owner became the proprietor of one of the parcels.

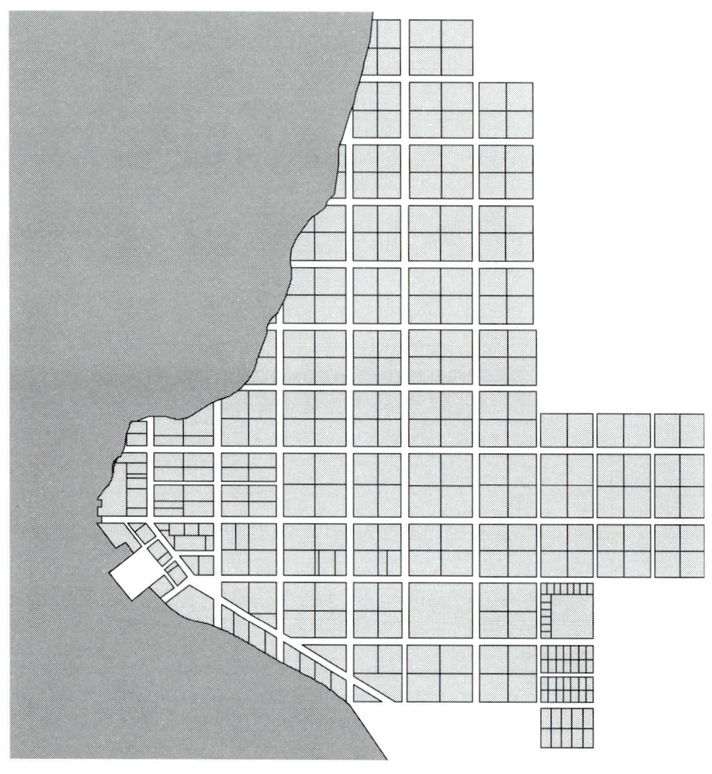

· 1829

The 1887 map shows the flexibility of the platting system to accommodate growth within the block. Property owners approved to parcel-off part of their own property for the sake of prosperity. This event in turn nurtured a residential population with a mix-of-incomes and, consequently, a variety of buildings types.

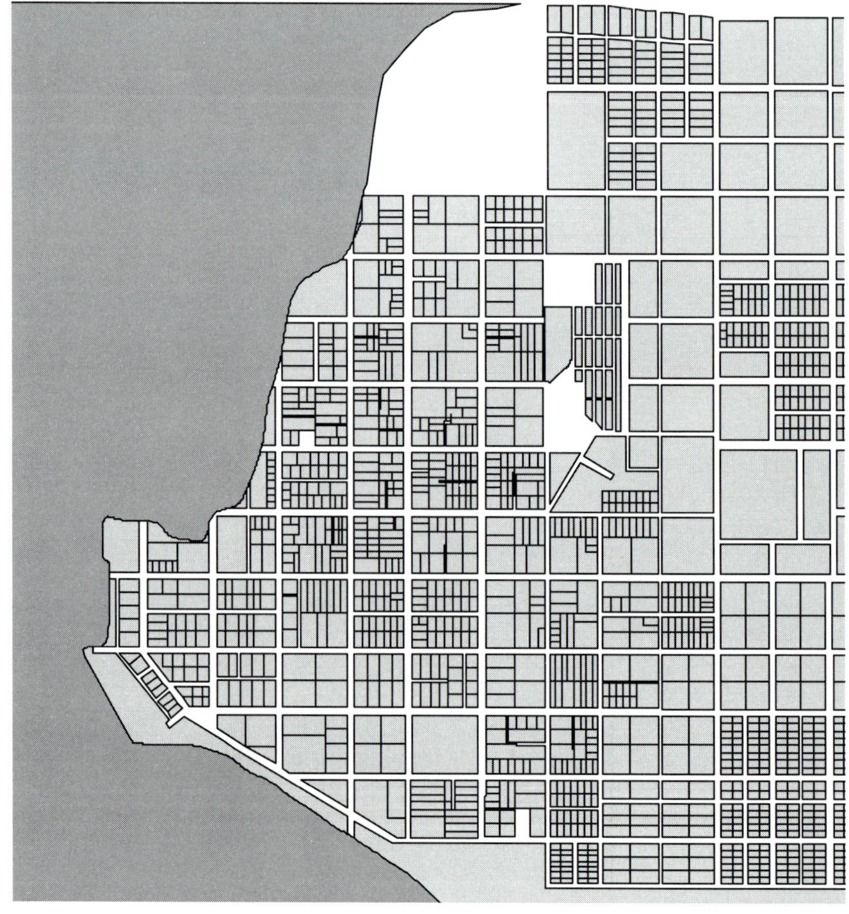

· 1887

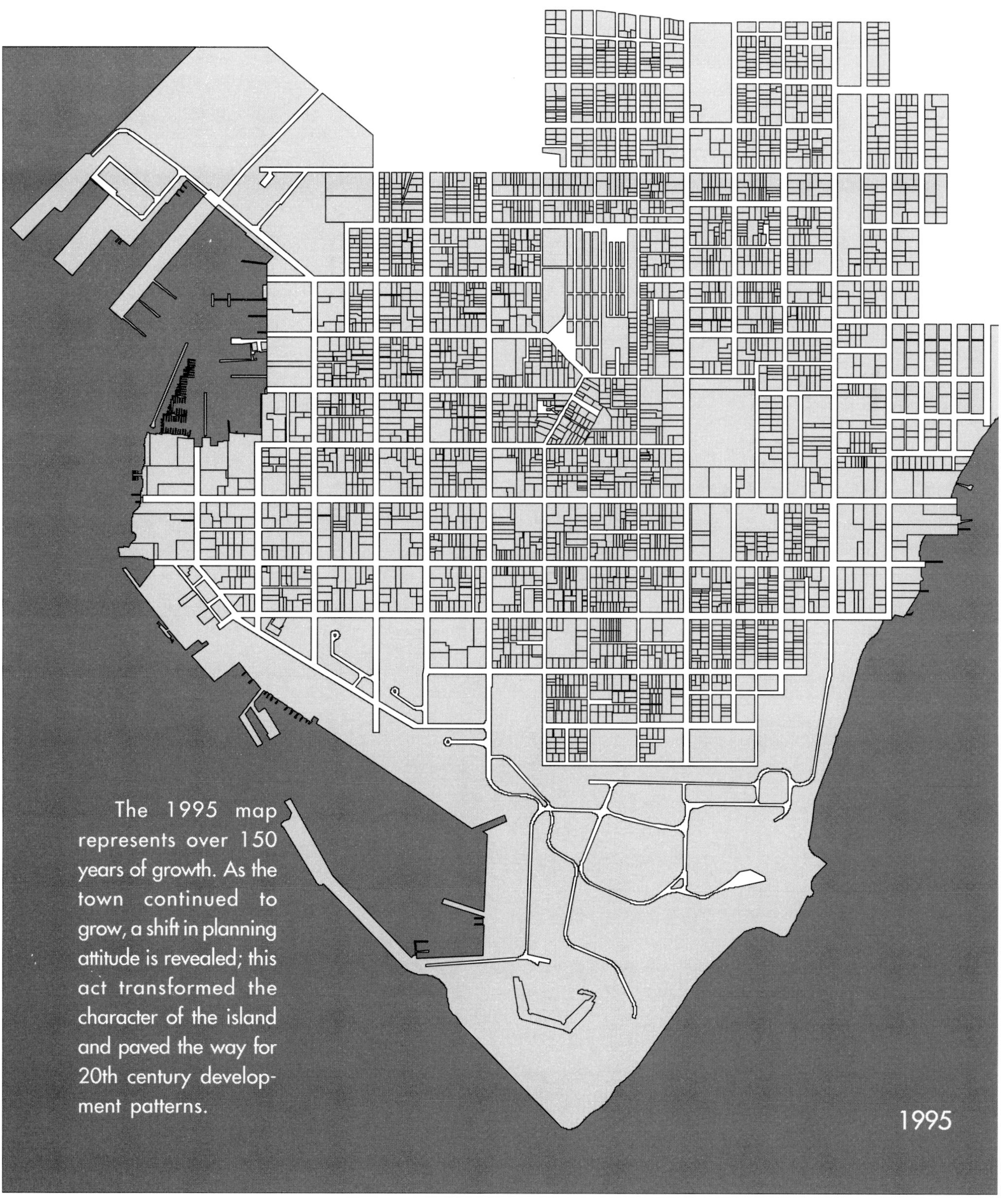

The 1995 map represents over 150 years of growth. As the town continued to grow, a shift in planning attitude is revealed; this act transformed the character of the island and paved the way for 20th century development patterns.

Town Layout:

The town was surveyed and mapped by William Whitehead, a civil engineer, in 1829. It was laid out as a square grid oriented at 45 degrees from the cardinal directions, and diagonal to compass points.

- The original plat extended from Front Street to Angela Street.
- Typical blocks measured 400 ft X 450 ft.
- The dimension of typical lots was 50 ft X 100 ft and 46 ft X 90 ft. The individual lots were subdivided later.
- The Right-Of-Way (distance from property line to facing property line) along the Duval Street is 60 ft.
- All other Right-Of-Ways measure 50 ft.

Town Character:

Key West has a collection of early 19th and 20th century buildings. The appearance, layout of the city and sense of identity was well established by the 1890's.

- Early drawings of Key West, depict it as a fishing village.
- A survey of the area recorded 64 blocks and two public squares, within 258 acres.
- By 1862, the town had 2,800 people, 800 stores, 20 warehouses, 4 churches, and 4 schools occupying 765 acres.

TYPICAL BLOCK

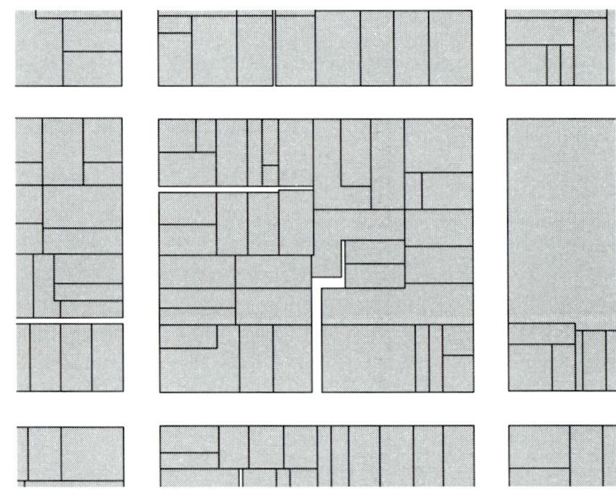

TYPICAL PLATTING

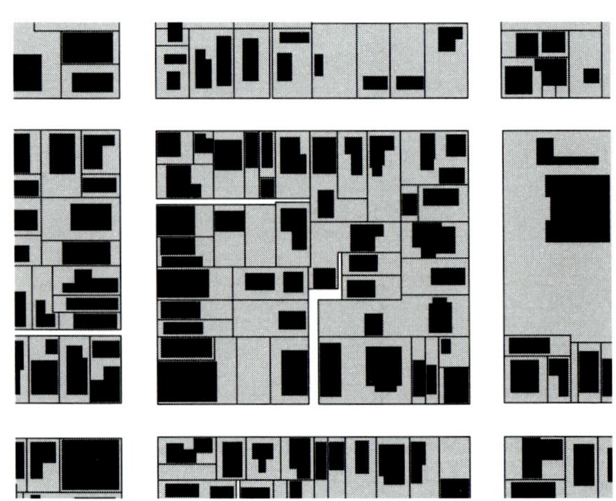

TYPICAL PLACEMENT

AMERICAN URBAN TYPOLOGIES

KEY WEST FLORIDA

ERICK VALLE

City Profile:

Location	: Longitude 82 , Latitude 24.5 degrees
Settled	: C. 1513 as a Spanish seaport
Founder	: Ponce de Leon
Climate	: Tropical
Tempature	: 70 degrees - January
	: 85 degrees - August
City Plan	: Historic district planned in 1822
Area	: 1.5 square miles
Population	: 10,000

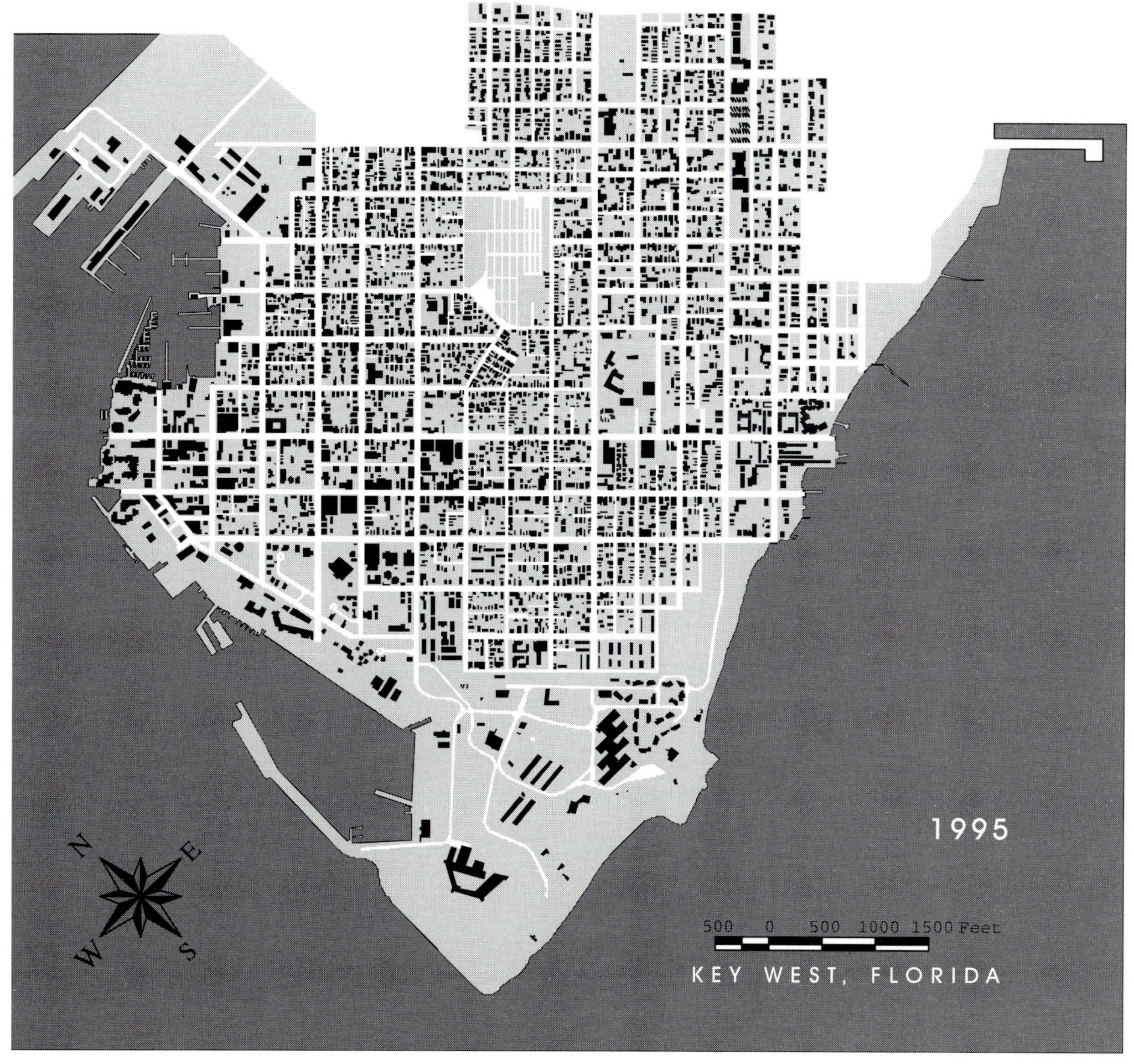

ARCHITECTURAL CHARACTERISTICS:

The basic features which distinguish the "Conch" architecture of Key West, include:

- Craftsmanship of wood details.
- Balloon frame construction.
- Raised foundations with crawl spaces.
- Incised or attached porches.
- Covered porches with turned balustrades and posts.
- Buildings of 1, 2, or 2 1/2 stories.
- Three to six bay facades.
- Main entry is directly off the sidewalk.
- Horizontal siding, weatherboards or clapboards.
- Tongue and groove porch flooring.
- 2/2 and 6/6 double hung slash windows.
- Vertically proportioned openings.
- Wood shutters.
- Roofs finished with metal shingles or V-crimp.
- Cisterns and outbuildings.
- White, light gray and pastel shades for exterior paint.
- Disciplined setbacks from the sidewalk.

Conch TEMPLE

Conch SHOTGUN

EXTENDED PORCHES

Architectural Precedents:

The Key West building stock is the result of shipbuilding practices adapted from the Caribbean and New England.

- Overhanging eaves covering extended porches, sloping gutters to funnel rainwater from down spouts to cisterns, spacious verandas, balustrades, wide exterior lapsiding, and louvered shutters (which allowed breezes to circulate) came from the Bahamas.
- Shotgun dwellings came from the Gulf Coast (originally West Africa and the French Caribbean) .
- Roof hatches (for ventilation) from ships.
- Well proportioned houses with 2/2 and 6/6 double hung sash windows, columns, and pediments came from the Northeast of the United States.

AIR VENTS

Conch Bahama

Conch Bungalow

Conch Sawtooth

Conch Captain

Conch Mansion

Conch Eyebrow

Conch Six-bay

Conch Temple

One-And-A-Half-Story

Conch Cottage

Conch Shotgun

Conch Four Square

Conch Guest House

CONCH SAWTOOTH:

This single family home is characterized by a porch running parallel to the street, a single-room footprint with a hallway and a comfortable private back yard. This building is very flexible and all its additions are incrementally attached to the main structure off the rear wing. The floor plan is organized around its central hall. It is raised on a pier foundation to allow for air circulation, flooding recharge and privacy. The building is setback from the front property line to allow for a semi-private front yard and additional privacy.

The common building name is: "Classical Revival Three-Bay."

CASE STUDIES:

ADDRESS : 737 Love Lane
: 1305 Petron Avenue
: 807 Fleming Avenue

STREET VIEW

TYPICAL BLOCK

Block Type:

BLOCK	: 400 ft X 350 ft
TOTAL LOTS	: 35
CORNER	: 8 ft radius

Street Type:

SPATIAL RATIO	: 1:4 (Height to Width)
R.O.W.	: 50 ft
LANE(S)	: Two lanes, two way
PARKING	: Parallel, two sides
SIDEWALK	: 10 ft, both sides
LANDSCAPE	: Tropical
STREETSCAPE	: Lamp post
SIGNAGE	: Posted on main structure
ELECTRICITY	: Overhead wiring
USE	: Mixed-Use
ORIENTATION	: Southeast

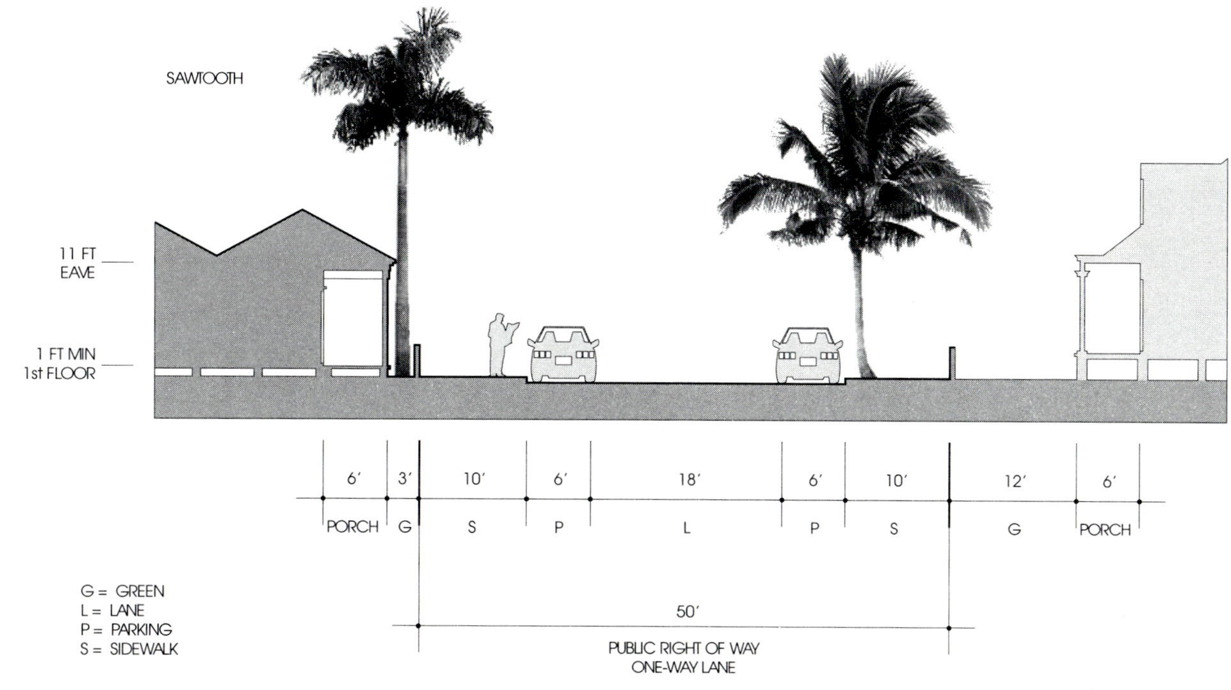

STREET SECTION THROUGH FLEMING STREET

LOT TYPE:

TYPE	: Rear yard
COVERAGE	: 50 %
F.A.R.	: 50 %
PERVIOUS AREA	: 65 %
SIZE	: 25 ft X 45 ft
PARKING	: Commonly none on site
FRONT YARD	: 8 ft
SIDE YARD	: 4 ft
REAR YARD	: 5 ft
ENCROACHMENT	: 5 ft maximum, with open structure
OUTBUILDING	: None
FENCE	: 4 ft high front and 6 ft high sides and rear
DRIVEWAY	: None

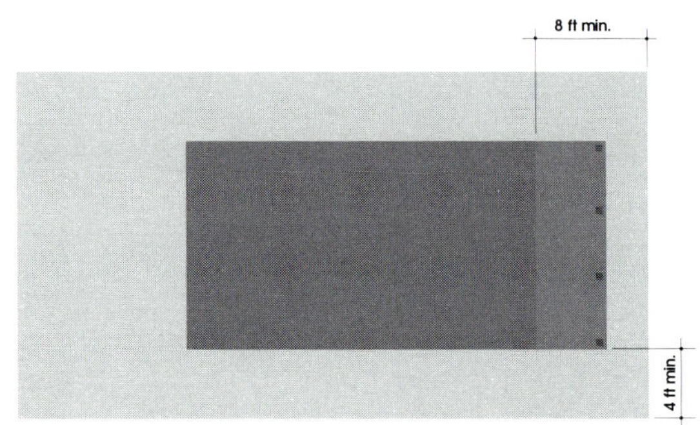

BUILDING LOT

LOCATION MAP

FRONT ELEVATION

BUILDING TYPE:

CONSTRUCTION	: Wood frame
USE	: Residential
UNITS/ACRE	: 38
FACADE ASPECT	: Porch
PORCH	: 5 ft
CLIMATE CONTROL	: Porch for screening the sun, air vents and double hung windows for natural ventilation
SECURITY	: Public rooms and main entrance off the sidewalk
WINDOW/DOOR	: Vertical proportions

BUILDING FINISH:

WALLS	: Wood horizontal siding
ROOF	: Metal shingles or V-crimp metal
COLOR	: White, light gray or pastel shades
PRIVACY	: Fences, raised floor and land-scaping

PEDESTRIAN VIEW

Plan Type:

CHARACTERISTIC	: Central hall
SHAPE	: Rectangular
FOOTPRINT	: 20 ft X 50 ft
SQUARE FOOTAGE	: 375 to 1000 sq ft
FIRST LEVEL	: 2.5 ft above the sidewalk
ORIENTATION	: Perpendicular to street
KITCHEN	: 1st floor, overlooking rear yard
DINING ROOM	: 1st floor, overlooking rear yard
LIVING ROOM	: 1st floor, overlooking sidewalk
BEDROOM(S)	: !st floor, overlooking rear yard
YARD	: Semi-public front, private rear
OUTBUILDING	: None

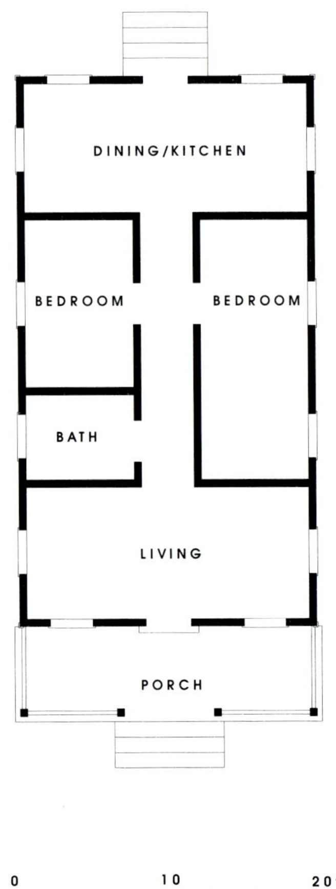

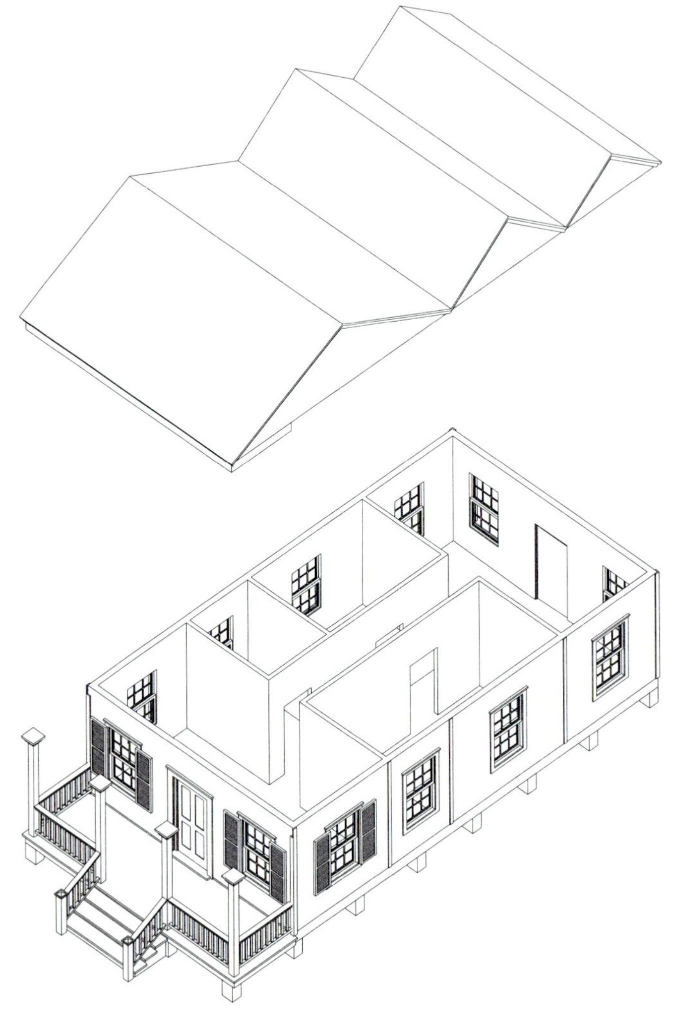

FLOOR PLAN(S)

THE URBAN AND LANDSCAPE REGULATIONS WERE DERIVED FROM AN ANALYSIS OF SANBORN MAPS, HISTORIC AMERICAN BUILDING SURVEYS, AERIALS, SITE VISITS, AND CONVERSATIONS WITH LOCAL RESIDENTS, HISTORIC PRESERVATION GROUPS, ARCHITECTS, LANDSCAPE ARCHITECTS, TRAFFIC ENGINEERS, SCHOOLS OF ARCHITECTURE AND PLANNING, AND ZONING DEPARTMENTS.

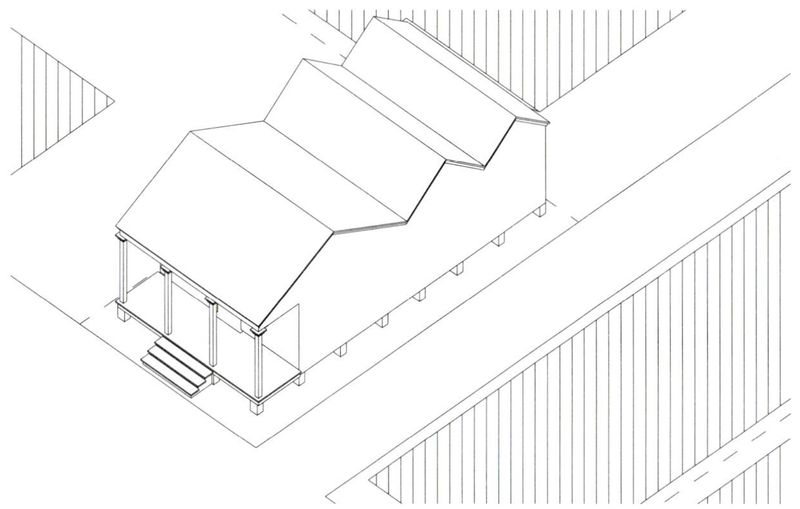

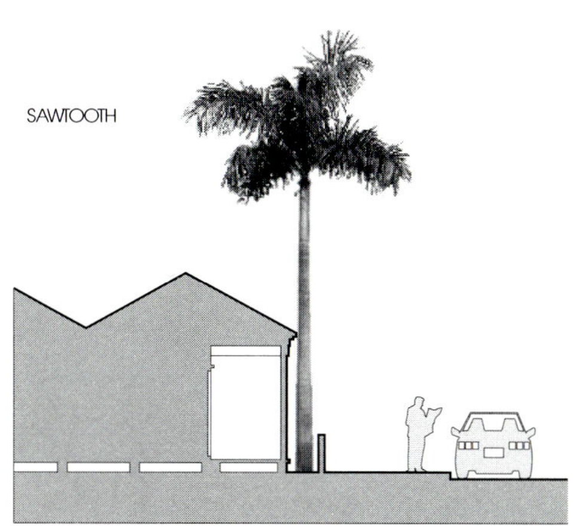

URBAN REGULATIONS

PLACEMENT

: 50 % MAXIMUM BUILDING LOT COVERAGE
: 65 % MINIMUM PERVIOUS AREA
: 30 % MINIMUM STREET FRONTAGE BUILD-OUT
: 8 FT MINIMUM FRONT YARD
: 4 FT MINIMUM SIDE STREET YARD
: 5 FT MINIMUM REAR YARD

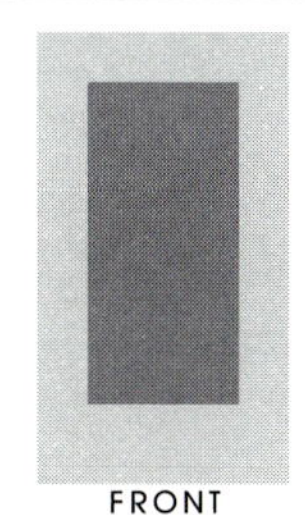

ENCROACHMENT

: 5 FT MAXIMUM DEPTH FRONT PORCH REQUIRED AND 100 % MINIMUM WIDTH

PARKING / OUTBUILDING

: NONE

HEIGHT & USE

: 11 FT MAXIMUM BUILDING EAVE
: FIRST FLOOR RESIDENTIAL

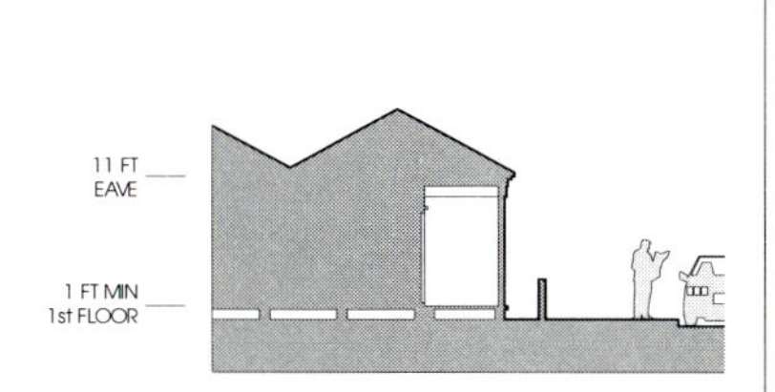

LANDSCAPE REGULATIONS

FRONT YARD

: *MAY BE PLANTED WITH SHRUBS, HEDGES, FLOWERS AND/OR GRASS*
: *LAWN AREA 30% MIN. OF THE LOT AREA*
: *VINES MAY BE PLANTED TO GROW ON PORCHES*

PERIMETER

: A CONTINUOUS HEDGE IS REQUIRED AT A MINIMUM OF 5 FT HEIGHT AT THE SIDES & REAR
: DEPENDING ON THE STREET TYPE, THE FRONT ELEVATION MAY BE SCREENED WITH TREES AND PALMS

DRIVEWAY

: NONE

RIGHT-OF-WAY

: MAY BE PLANTED WITH PALMS AND TREES
: UNPAVED AREAS SHALL BE PLANTED WITH GRASS

CONCH SHOTGUN:

This building type is a single family home with a porch running perpendicular to the street, a footprint that is a single room wide plus hallway and a comfortable side yard for on-site parking. It was commonly used to house cigar-makers. The plan is organized around a hallway that runs the entire depth on one side. The building is raised on a pier foundation to allow for air circulation, flooding recharge and privacy. It is commonly found in clusters of 4 to 6 with a side yard on some to allow for on-site parking.

This building is commonly known as a "Three-Bay Shotgun House or Cigar-Maker Shack."

CASE STUDIES:

ADDRESS
: 413 Truman Avenue
: 322 Simonton Street
: 1103 Fleming Street
: 822 Olivia Street

STREET VIEW

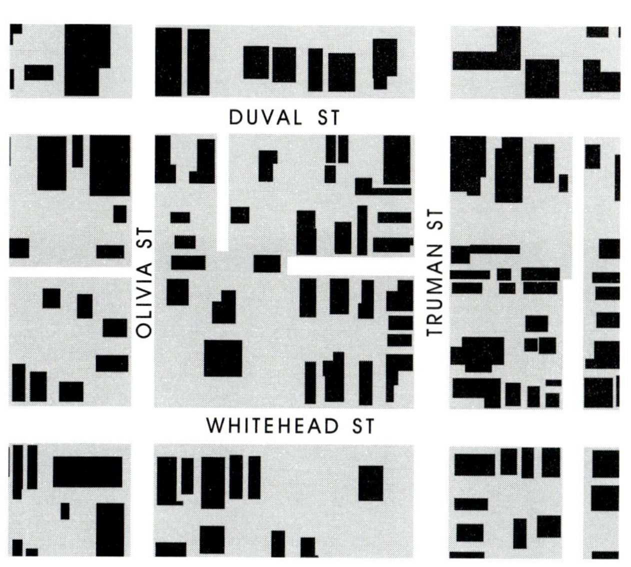

BLOCK

Block Type:

BLOCK	: 380 ft X 350 ft
TOTAL LOTS	: 23
CORNER	: 8 ft *radius*

Street Type:

SPATIAL RATIO	: 1:3 (Height to Width)
R.O.W.	: 35 ft
LANE(S)	: Two lanes, one way
PARKING	: None
SIDEWALK	: 4 ft one side and 6 ft one side
LANDSCAPE	: Tropical
STREETSCAPE	: Lamp post
SIGNAGE	: Posted on main structure
ELECTRICITY	: Overhead wiring
USE	: Mixed-Use
ORIENTATION	: Southeast

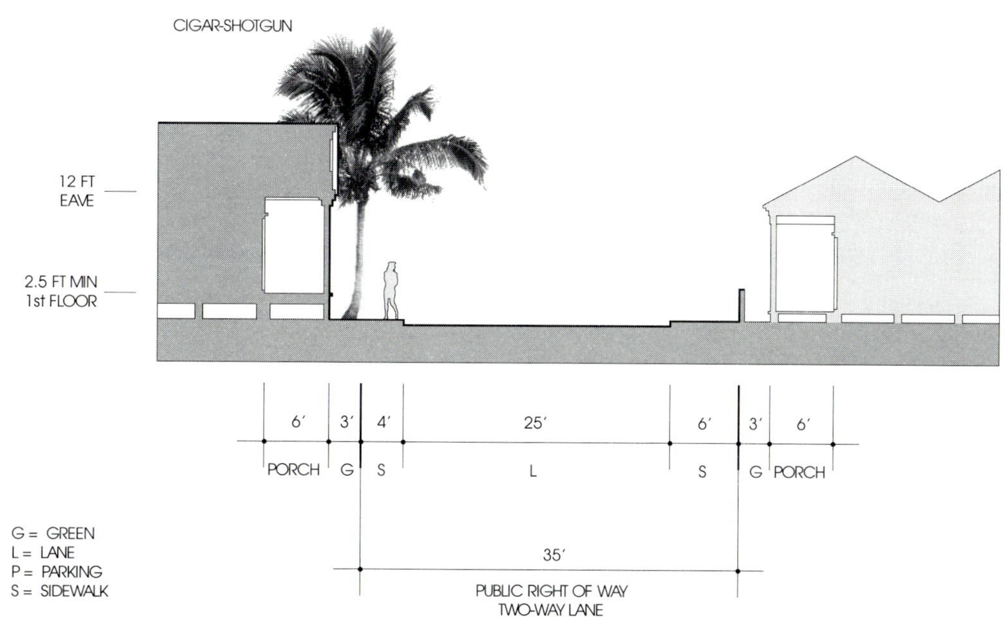

STREET SECTION THROUGH TRUMAN AVENUE

Lot Type:

TYPE	: Rear yard
COVERAGE	: 40 %
F.A.R.	: 40 %
PERVIOUS AREA	: 65 %
SIZE	: 25 ft X 45 ft
PARKING	: One car parking on site
FRONT YARD	: 8 ft
SIDE YARD	: 2 ft
REAR YARD	: 5 ft
ENCROACHMENT	: 4 ft maximum, with open structure
OUTBUILDING	: None
FENCE	: 4 ft high front and 6 ft high sides and rear
DRIVEWAY	: Width 10 ft maximum, perpendicular to street

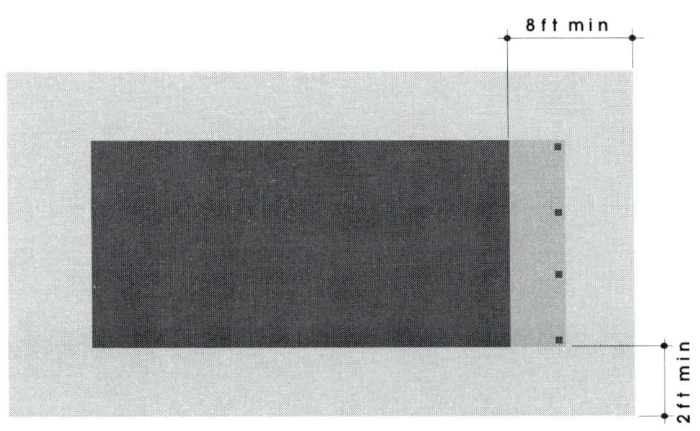

BUILDING LOT

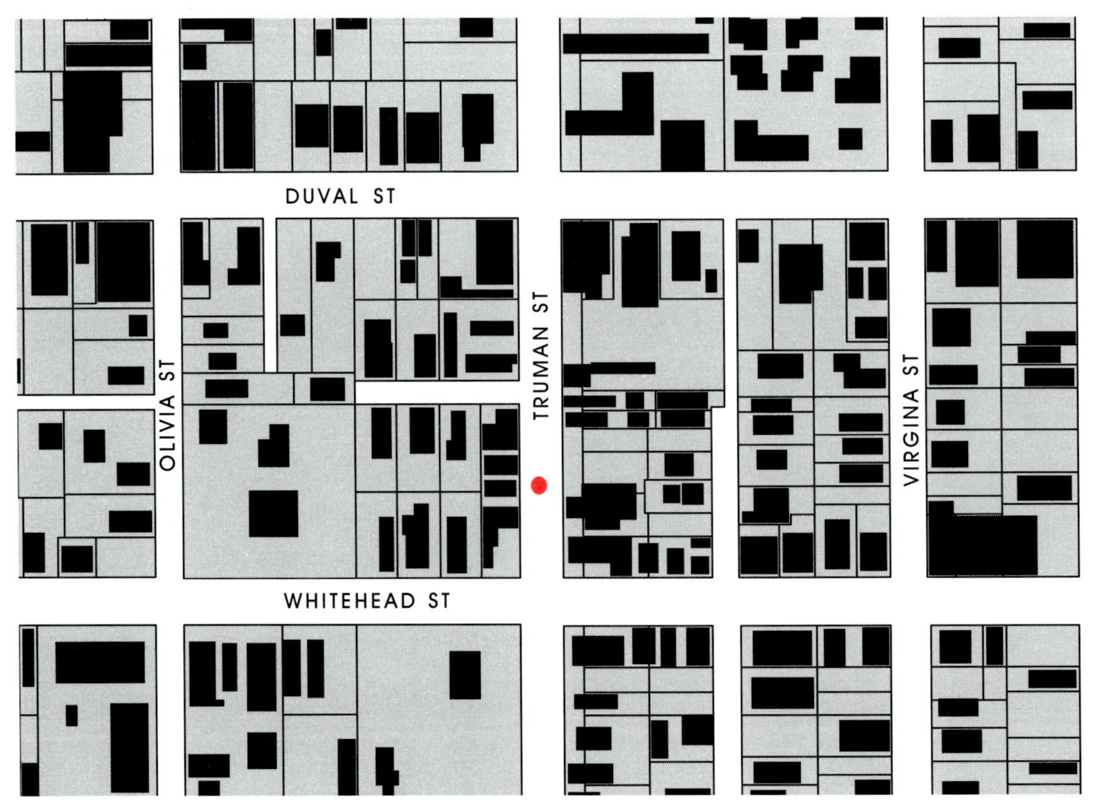

LOCATION MAP

FRONT ELEVATION

Building Type:

CONSTRUCTION	: Wood frame
USE	: Residential
UNITS/ACRE	: 38
FACADE ASPECT	: Porch
PORCH	: 4 ft
CLIMATE CONTROL	: Porch for screening the sun, air vents and double hung windows for natural ventilation
SECURITY	: Public rooms and main entrance off the sidewalk
WINDOW/DOOR	: Vertical proportions

Building Finish:

WALLS	: Wood horizontal siding
ROOF	: Metal shingles or V-crimp metal
COLOR	: White, light gray or pastel shades
PRIVACY	: Fences, raised floor and land-scaping

PEDESTRIAN VIEW

PLAN TYPE:

CHARACTERISTIC	: Side hall
SHAPE	: Rectangular
FOOTPRINT	: 18 ft X 30 ft
SQUARE FOOTAGE	: 450 to 600 sq ft
FIRST LEVEL	: 2 ft above the sidewalk
ORIENTATION	: Perpendicular to street
KITCHEN	: 1st floor, overlooking rear yard
DINING ROOM	: 1st floor, overlooking rear yard
LIVING ROOM	: 1st floor, overlooking sidewalk
BEDROOM(S)	: 1st floor, overlooking side yard
YARD	: Semi-public front, private rear
OUTBUILDING	: None

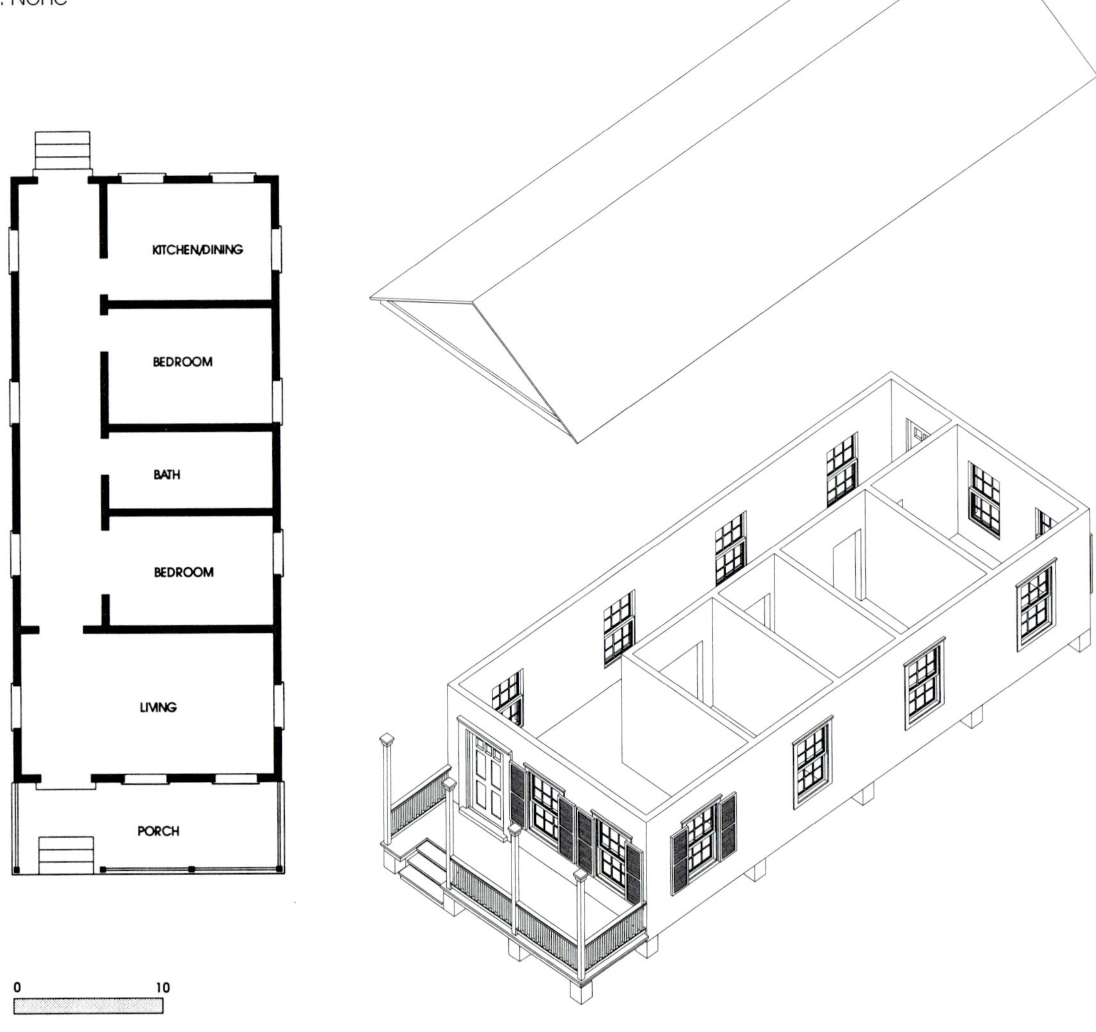

FLOOR PLAN(S)

THE URBAN AND LANDSCAPE REGULATIONS WERE DERIVED FROM AN ANALYSIS OF SANDBORN MAPS, HISTORIC AMERICAN BUILDING SURVEYS, AERIALS, SITE VISITS, AND CONVERSATIONS WITH LOCAL RESIDENTS, HISTORIC PRESERVATION GROUPS, ARCHITECTS, LANDSCAPE ARCHITECTS, TRAFFIC ENGINEERS, SCHOOLS OF ARCHITECTURE AND PLANNING, AND ZONING DEPARTMENTS.

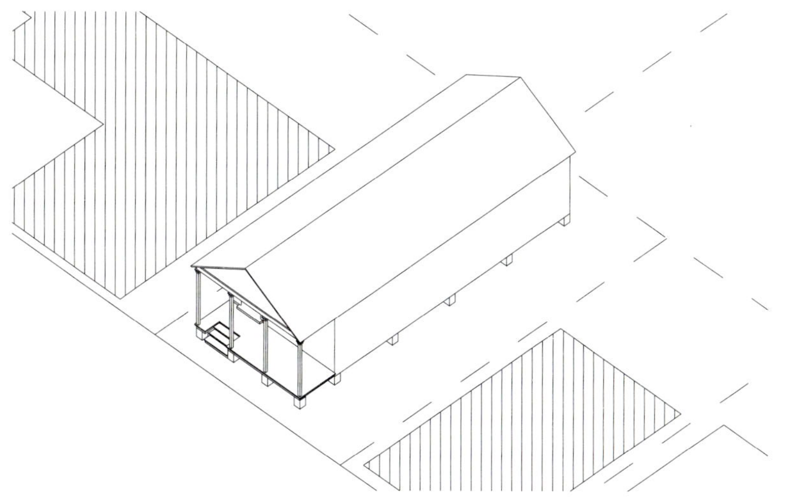

URBAN REGULATIONS

PLACEMENT

: 40 % MAXIMUM BUILDING LOT COVERAGE
: 65 % MINIMUM PERVIOUS AREA
: 60 % MINIMUM STREET FRONTAGE BUILD-OUT
: 8 FT MINIMUM FRONT YARD
: 2 FT MINIMUM SIDE STREET YARD
: 5 FT MINIMUM REAR YARD

ENCROACHMENT

: 4 FT MINIMUM DEPTH FRONT PORCH REQUIRED AND 100% MINIMUM WIDTH

PARKING / OUTBUILDING

: ONE CAR SPACE ALLOWED
: 2 FT MINIMUM SIDES SETBACK

HEIGHT & USE

: 12 FT MAXIMUM BUILDING EAVE
: FIRST FLOOR RESIDENTIAL

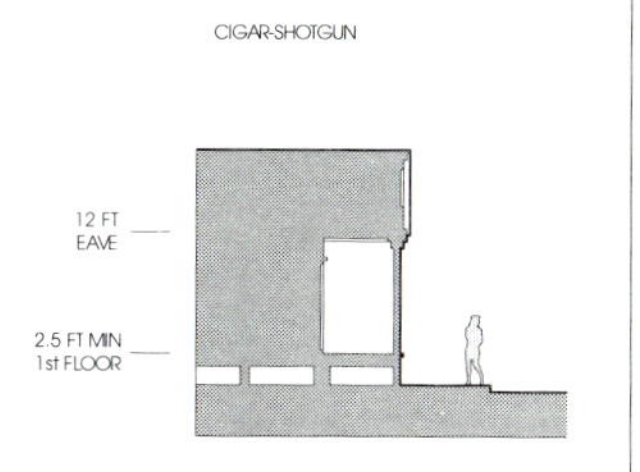

LANDSCAPE REGULATIONS

FRONT YARD

: *MAY BE PLANTED WITH SHRUBS, HEDGES, FLOWERS AND/OR GRASS*
: *LAWN AREA MAY BE A MINIMUM OF 30 % OF THE TOTAL LOT AREA*
: *VINES MAY BE PLANTED TO GROW ON PORCHES*

PERIMETER

: A CONTINUOUS HEDGE IS REQUIRED AT A MINIMUM OF 5 FT HEIGHT AT THE SIDES & REAR
: DEPENDING ON THE STREET TYPE, THE FRONT ELEVATION MAY BE SCREENED WITH TREES AND PALMS

DRIVEWAY

: MAY BE PLANTED WITH SHRUBS, HEDGES, FLOWERS AND/OR GRASS
: MAY BE A MAXIMUM OF 12 FT IN WIDTH
: SHALL BE A STRAIGHT, PERPENDICULAR PAVED AREA RUNNING FROM THE STREET TO PARKING

RIGHT-OF-WAY

: MAY BE PLANTED WITH PALMS AND TREES
: UNPAVED AREAS SHALL BE PLANTED WITH GRASS

Conch Bungalow:

This single family home has a porch along the front, a two room wide footprint plus a hallway, a comfortable rear yard and a side yard used for on-site parking. The plan is organized around a central hall that spans its entire depth. The building is raised on a pier foundation to allow for air circulation, flooding recharge and privacy. It is setback from the front property line creating a semi-private front yard and additional privacy.

This building is commonly known as a "Bungalow."

Case Study:

ADDRESS : 1401 Truman Avenue

STREET VIEW

PEARL ST
ALBURY ST
TRUMAN AVE
FLORIDA ST

BLOCK

Block Type:

BLOCK	: 290 ft X 160 ft
TOTAL LOTS	: 9
CORNER	: 8 ft radius

Street Type:

SPATIAL RATIO	: 1:3 (Height to Width)
R.O.W.	: 50 ft
LANE(S)	: Two lanes, two way
PARKING	: Parallel, one side
SIDEWALK	: 10 ft, both sides
LANDSCAPE	: Tropical
STREETSCAPE	: Lamp post
SIGNAGE	: Posted on main structure
ELECTRICITY	: Overhead wiring
USE	: Residential
ORIENTATION	: Southeast

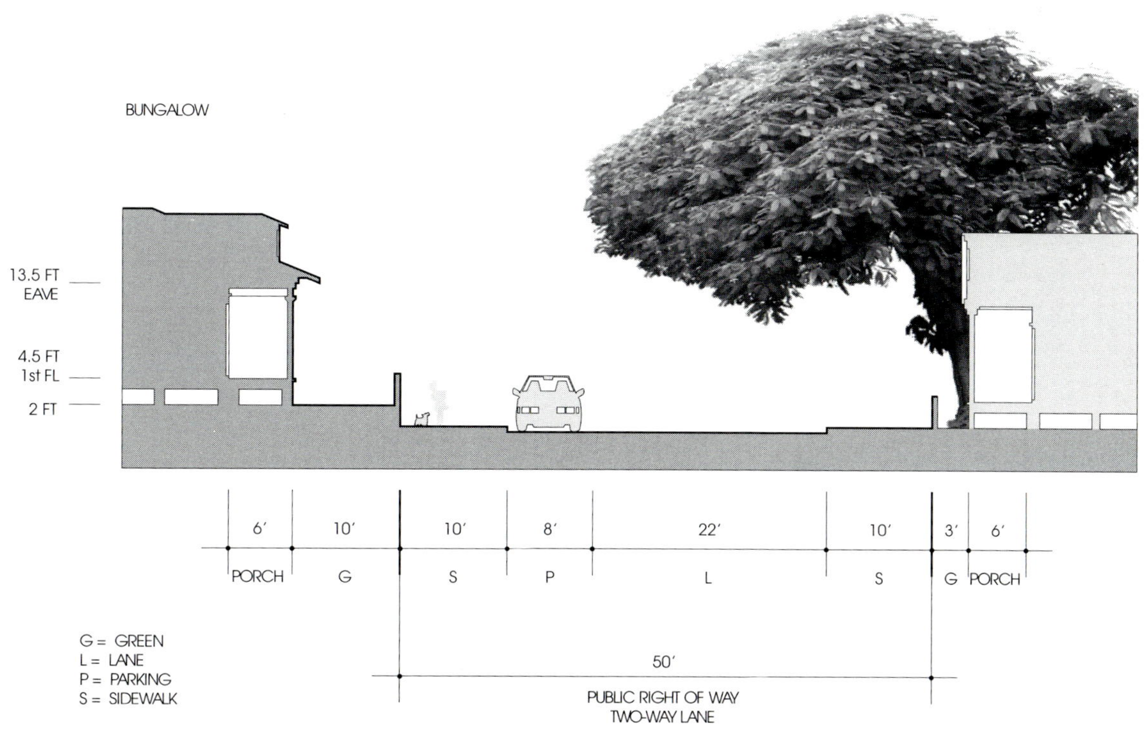

STREET SECTION THROUGH TRUMAN AVENUE

LOT TYPE:

TYPE : Rear yard

COVERAGE : 20 %

F.A.R. : 40 %

PERVIOUS AREA : 65 %

SIZE : 50 ft X 95 ft

PARKING : Two car parking on site

FRONT YARD : 16 ft

SIDE YARD : 5 ft

REAR YARD : 30 ft

ENCROACHMENT : 5 ft maximum, with open structure

OUTBUILDING : Rear yard

FENCE : 4 ft high front and 6 ft high sides and rear

DRIVEWAY : Width 12 ft maximum, perpendicular to street

16 ft min

4 ft min.

BUILDING LOT

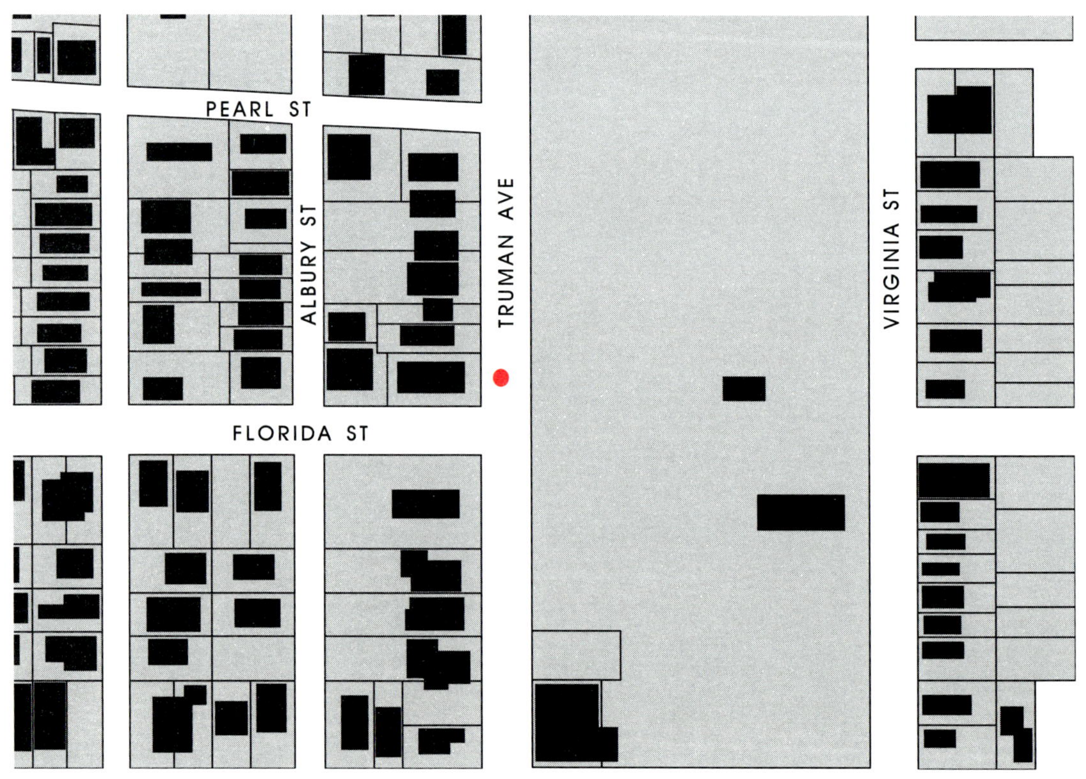

LOCATION MAP

FRONT ELEVATION

Building Type:

CONSTRUCTION	: Wood frame
USE	: Residential
UNITS/ACRE	: 9
FACADE ASPECT	: Porch
PORCH	: 5 ft
CLIMATE CONTROL	: Porch for screening the sun, air vents and double hung windows for natural ventilation
SECURITY	: Public rooms and main entrance off the sidewalk
WINDOW/DOOR	: Vertical proportions

Building Finish:

WALLS	: Wood horizontal siding
ROOF	: Metal shingles or V-crimp metal
COLOR	: White, light gray or pastel shades
PRIVACY	: Fences, raised floor and land-scaping

PEDESTRIAN VIEW

Plan Type:

CHARACTERISTIC	: Central hall
SHAPE	: Rectangular
FOOTPRINT	: 22 ft X 32 ft
SQUARE FOOTAGE	: 800 to 1000 sq ft
FIRST LEVEL	: 2.5 ft above the sidewalk
ORIENTATION	: Perpedicular to main street
KITCHEN	: 1st floor, overlooking rear yard
DINING ROOM	: 1st floor, overlooking rear yard
LIVING ROOM	: 1st floor, overlooking sidewalk
BEDROOM(S)	: 1st floor, overlooking side yard
YARD	: Semi-public front, private rear
OUTBUILDING	: In the rear yard

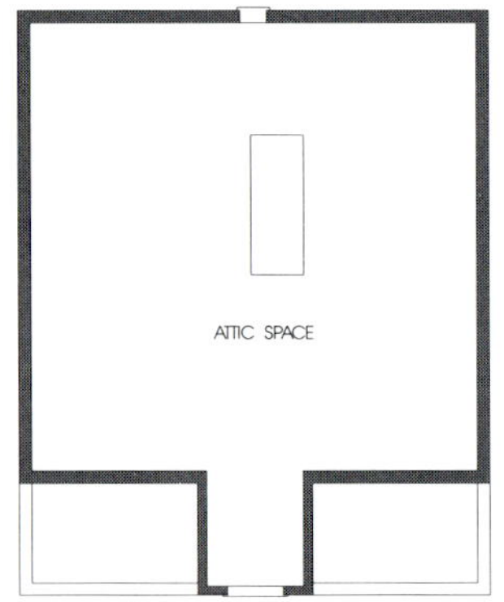

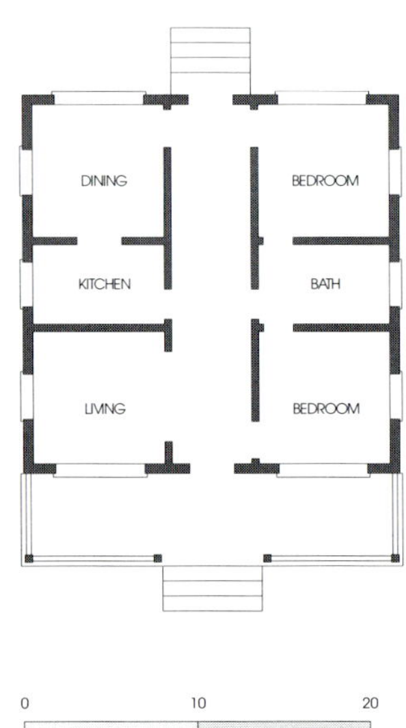

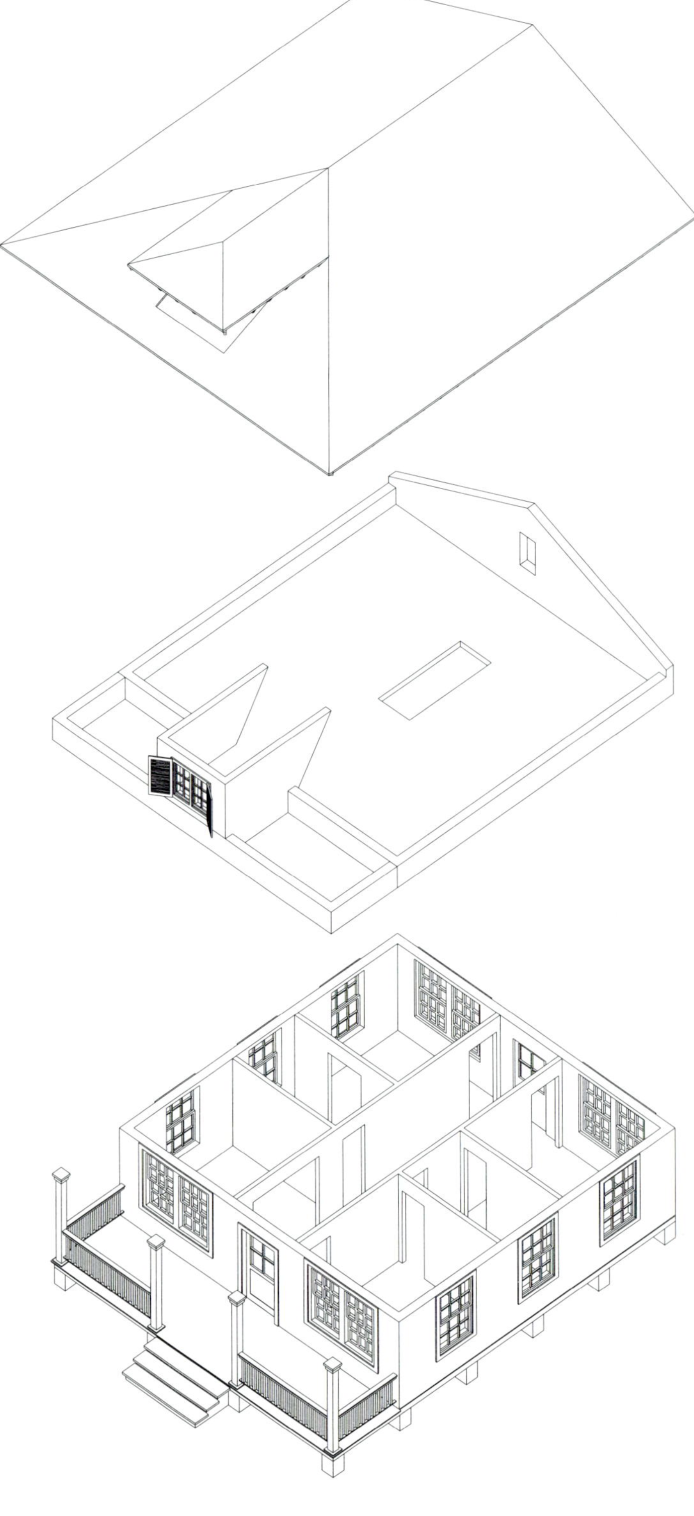

FLOOR PLAN(S)

THE URBAN AND LANDSCAPE REGULATIONS WERE DERIVED FROM AN ANALYSIS OF SANDBORN MAPS, HISTORIC AMERICAN BUILDING SURVEYS, AERIALS, SITE VISITS, AND CONVERSATIONS WITH LOCAL RESIDENTS, HISTORIC PRESERVATION GROUPS, ARCHITECTS, LANDSCAPE ARCHITECTS, TRAFFIC ENGINEERS, SCHOOLS OF ARCHITECTURE AND PLANNING , AND ZONING DEPARTMENTS.

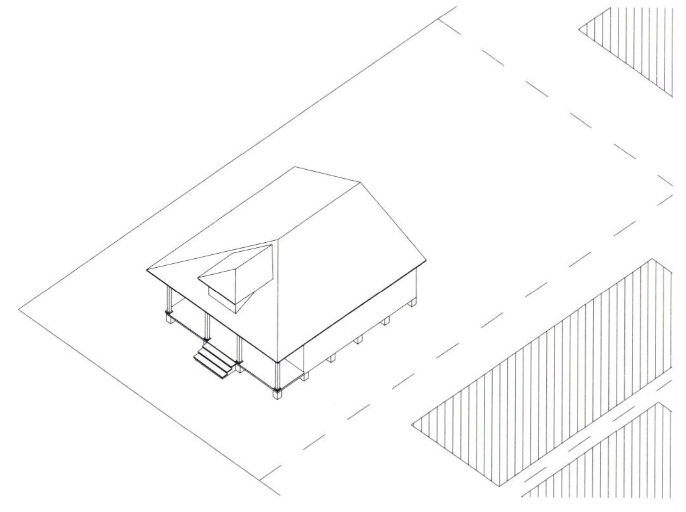

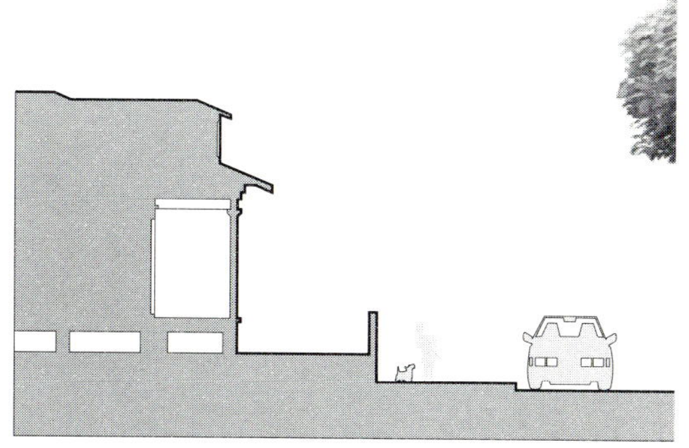

URBAN REGULATIONS

PLACEMENT

: 20 % MAXIMUM BUILDING LOT COVERAGE
: 65 % MINIMUM PERVIOUS AREA
: 70 % MINIMUM STREET FRONTAGE BUILD-OUT
: 16 FT MINIMUM FRONT YARD
: 5 FT MINIMUM SIDE YARDS
: 30 FT MINIMUM REAR YARD

ENCROACHMENT

: 5 FT MAXIMUM DEPTH FRONT PORCH REQUIRED AND 100% MINIMUM WIDTH

PARKING / OUTBUILDING

: TWO CAR SPACE ALLOWED
: 20 FT X 20 FT MAXIMUM
: 5 FT MINIMUM SIDES AND REAR SETBACK

HEIGHT & USE

: 13.5 FT MAXIMUM BUILDING EAVE
: FIRST FLOOR RESIDENTIAL

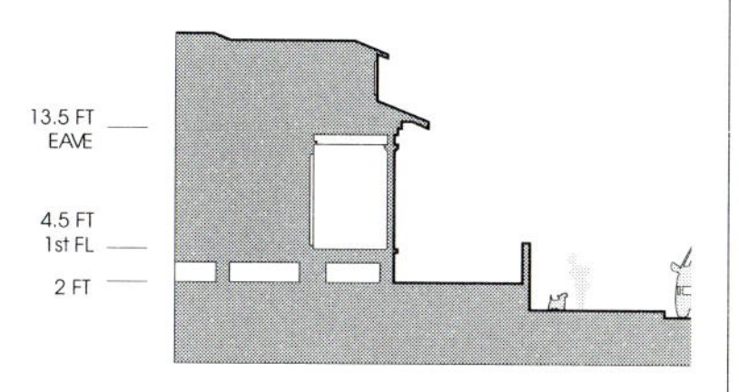

LANDSCAPE REGULATIONS

FRONT YARD

: *MAY BE PLANTED WITH SHRUBS, HEDGES, FLOWERS AND/OR GRASS*
: *LAWN AREA 30% MINIMUM OF THE TOTAL LOT AREA*
: *VINES MAY BE PLANTED TO GROW ON PORCHES*

PERIMETER

: A CONTINUOUS HEDGE IS REQUIRED AT A MINIMUM OF 6 FT HEIGHT AT THE SIDES & REAR
: DEPENDING ON THE STREET TYPE, THE FRONT ELEVATION MAY BE SCREENED WITH TREES AND PALMS

DRIVEWAY

: MAY BE PLANTED WITH SHRUBS, HEDGES, FLOWERS AND/OR GRASS
: 20 FT MAXIMUM IN WIDTH
: SHALL BE A STRAIGHT, PERPENDICULAR PAVED AREA RUNNING FROM THE STREET TO PARKING

RIGHT-OF-WAY

: MAY BE PLANTED WITH PALMS AND TREES
: UNPAVED AREAS SHALL BE PLANTED WITH GRASS

Conch One-And-A-Half-Story:

This building type is a single family one-and-a-half-story home with its front running perpendicular to the street, a one room wide footprint with a side hallway, a comfortable private back yard and on-site parking. The plan is organized along a side hallway. The building is raised on a pier foundation to allow for air circulation, flooding recharge and privacy. It is setback from the front property line creating a semi-private front yard and additional privacy.

The common building name is a Classic Revival Three Bay, Side Hall.

Case Studies:

ADDRESS	: 401 Francis Street
	: 1221 Petronia Street
	: 525 Margaret Street
	: 1025 Fleming Street
	: 614 Grinnel Street
	: 1115 Southard Street

STREET VIEW

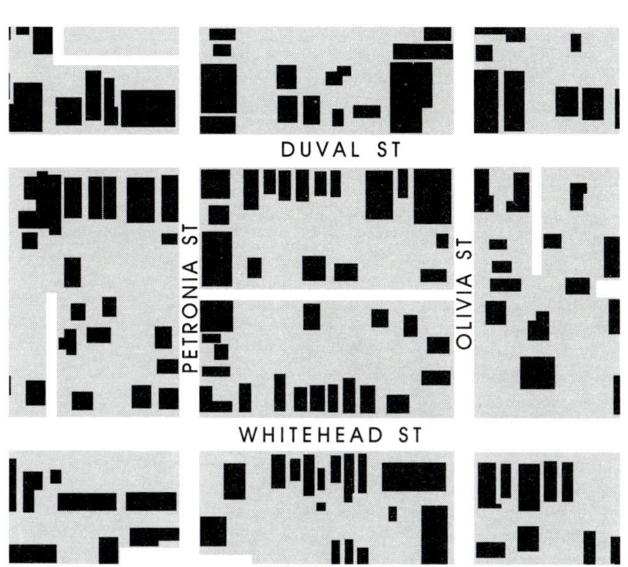

BLOCK

Block Type:

BLOCK	: 380 ft X 380 ft
TOTAL LOTS	: 38
CORNER	: 8 ft radius

Street Type:

SPATIAL RATIO	: 1:2 (Height to Width)
R.O.W.	: 32 ft
LANE(S)	: One lane, one way
PARKING	: Parallel, one side
SIDEWALK	: 6 ft, both sides
LANDSCAPE	: Tropical
STREETSCAPE	: Lamp post
SIGNAGE	: Posted on main structure
ELECTRICITY	: Overhead wiring
USE	: Mixed-Use
ORIENTATION	: Southeast

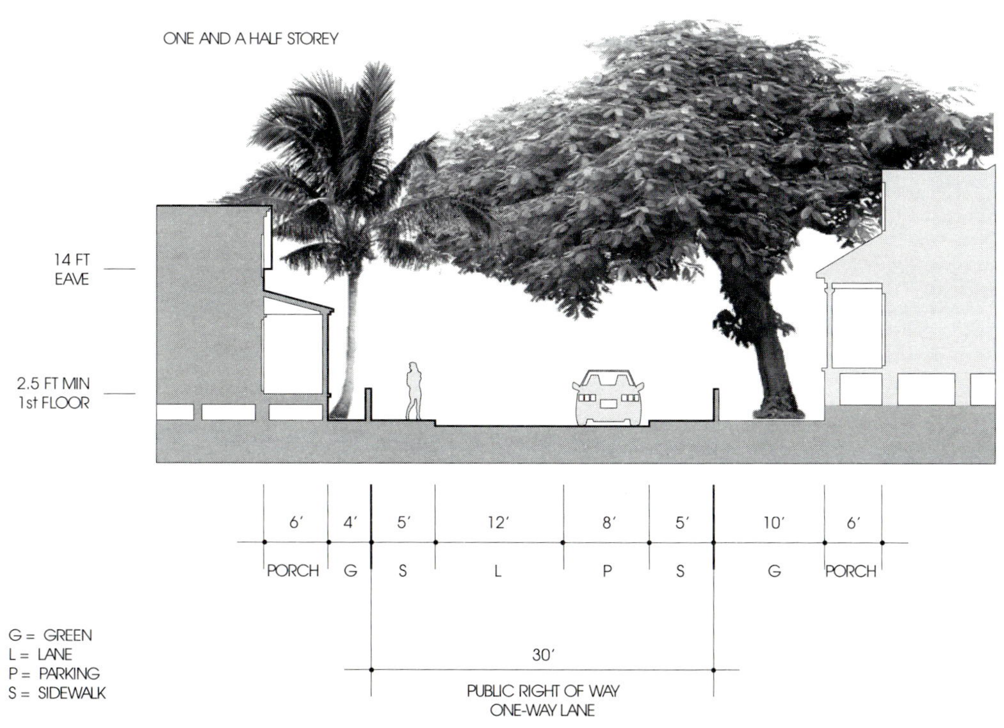

6′	4′	5′	12′	8′	5′	10′	6′
PORCH	G	S	L	P	S	G	PORCH

30′
PUBLIC RIGHT OF WAY
ONE-WAY LANE

G = GREEN
L = LANE
P = PARKING
S = SIDEWALK

STREET SECTION THROUGH WHITEHEAD STREET

LOT TYPE:

TYPE	: Rear yard
COVERAGE	: 25 %
F.A.R.	: 28 %
PERVIOUS AREA	: 65 %
SIZE	: 40 ft X 85 ft
PARKING	: None
FRONT YARD	: 10 ft
SIDE YARD	: 5 ft
REAR YARD	: 25 ft
ENCROACHMENT	: 5 ft maximum, with open structure
OUTBUILDING	: None
FENCE	: 4 ft high front and 6 ft high sides and rear
DRIVEWAY	: None

BUILDING LOT

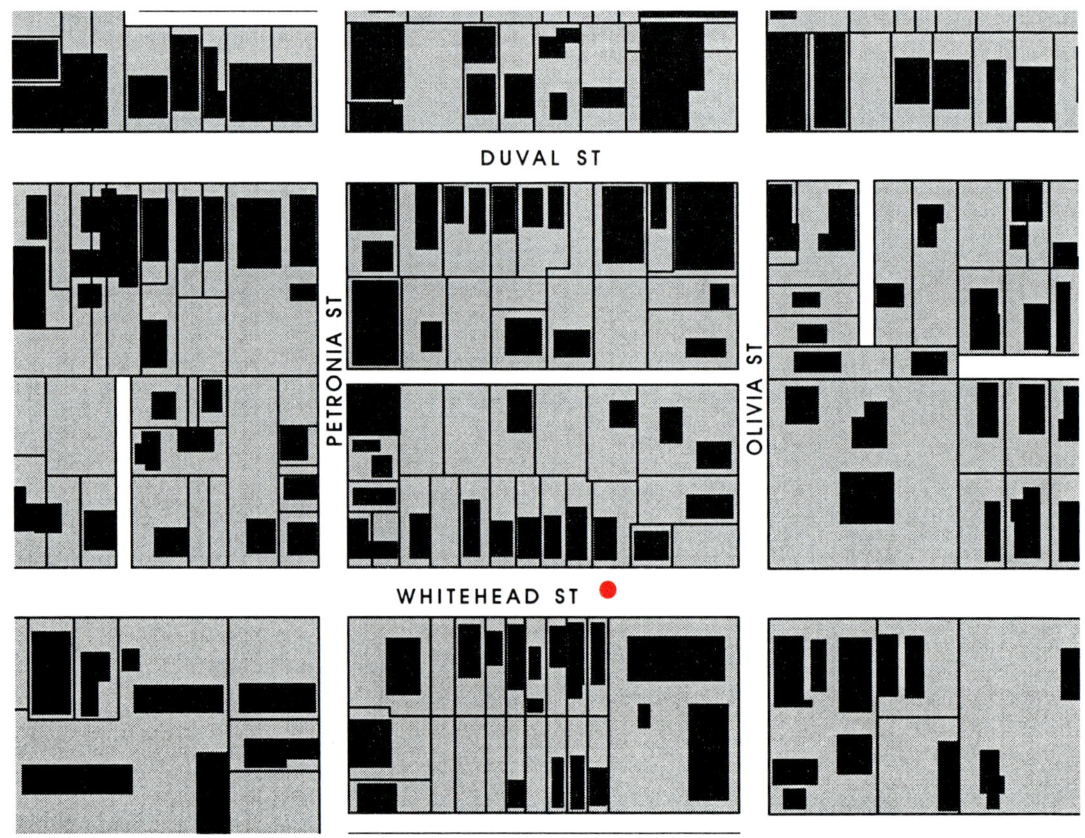

LOCATION MAP

FRONT ELEVATION

BUILDING TYPE:

CONSTRUCTION	: Wood frame
USE	: Residential
UNITS/ACRE	: 13.6
FACADE ASPECT	: Porch
PORCH	: 5 ft
CLIMATE CONTROL	: Porch for screening the sun, air vents and double hung windows for natural ventilation
SECURITY	: Public rooms and main entrance off the sidewalk
WINDOW/DOOR	: Vertical proportions

BUILDING FINISH:

WALLS	: Wood siding
ROOF	: Galvanized metal
COLORS	: White and green shutters
PRIVACY	: Fences, raised floor and landscaping

PEDESTRIAN VIEW

PLAN TYPE:

CHARACTERISTIC	: Central hall
SHAPE	: Rectangular
FOOTPRINT	: 15 ft X 30 ft
SQUARE FOOTAGE	: 750 - 900 sq ft
1ST LEVEL	: 2.5 ft above the sidewalk
ORIENTATION	: Perpendicular to the street
KITCHEN	: 1st floor, overlooking rear yard
DINING ROOM	: 1st floor, overlooking rear yard
LIVING ROOM	: 1st floor, overlooking sidewalk
BEDROOM(S)	: 1st & 2nd floors
YARD	: Private rear
OUTBUILDING	: None

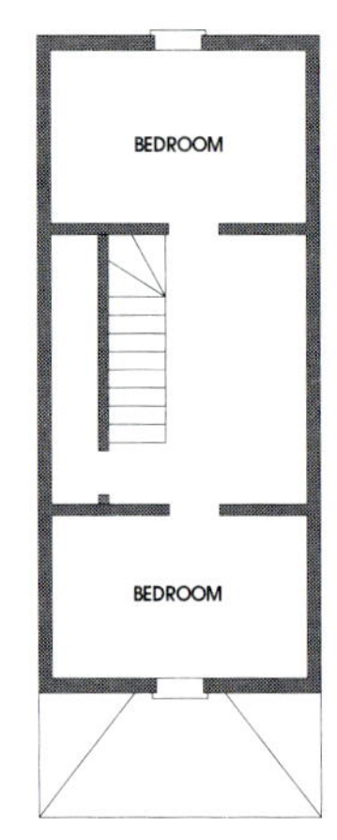

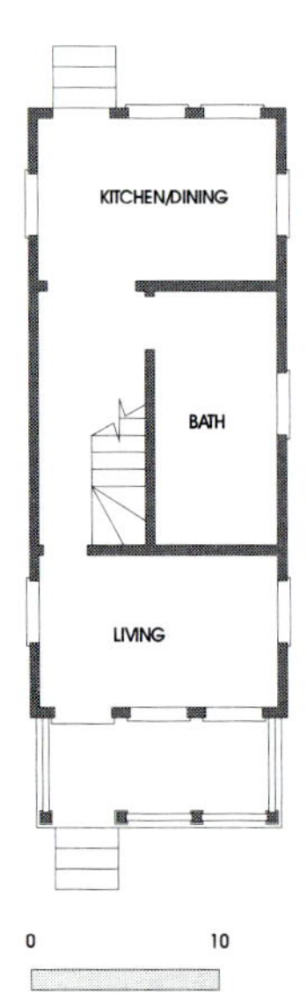

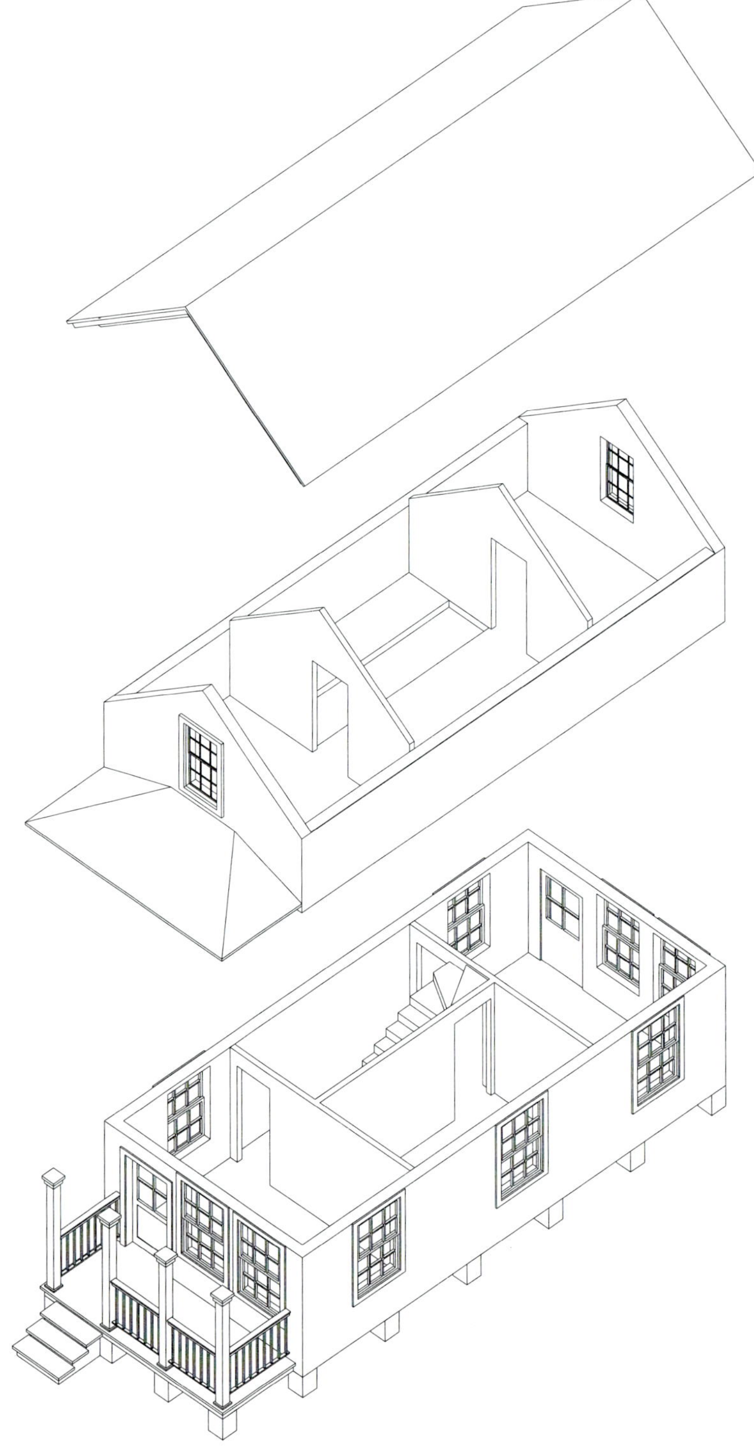

FLOOR PLANS

THE URBAN AND LANDSCAPE REGULATIONS WERE DERIVED FROM AN ANALYSIS OF SANDBORN MAPS, HISTORIC AMERICAN BUILDING SURVEYS, AERIALS, SITE VISITS, AND CONVERSATIONS WITH LOCAL RESIDENTS, HISTORIC PRESERVATION GROUPS, ARCHITECTS, LANDSCAPE ARCHITECTS, TRAFFIC ENGINEERS, SCHOOLS OF ARCHITECTURE AND PLANNING, AND ZONING DEPARTMENTS.

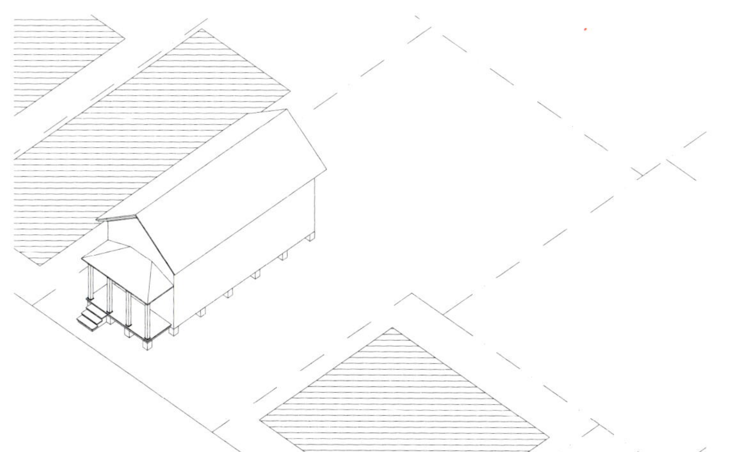

URBAN REGULATIONS

PLACEMENT

: 25 % MAXIMUM BUILDING LOT COVERAGE
: 65% MINIMUM PERVIOUS AREA
: 40 % MINIMUM STREET FRONTAGE BUILD-OUT
: 10 FT MINIMUM FRONT YARD
: 5 FT MINIMUM SIDE YARD
: 25 FT MINIMUM REAR YARD

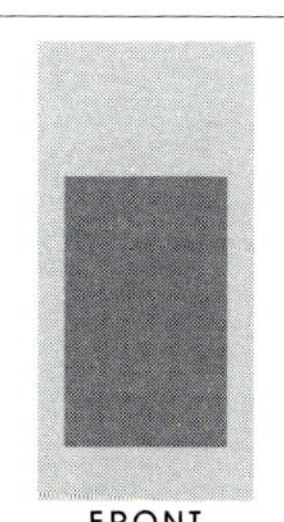

ENCROACHMENT

: 5 FT MINIMUM DEPTH FRONT PORCH REQUIRED AND 90% MINIMUM WIDTH

PARKING / OUTBUILDING

: ONE CAR SPACE ALLOWED
: 2 FT MINIMUM SIDE YARD
: 20 FT MAXIMUM DEPTH

HEIGHT & USE

: 16 FT MAXIMUM MAIN BUILDING EAVE
: 12 FT MAXIMUM PORCH EAVE
: FIRST FLOOR RESIDENTIAL
: SECOND FLOOR RESIDENTIAL

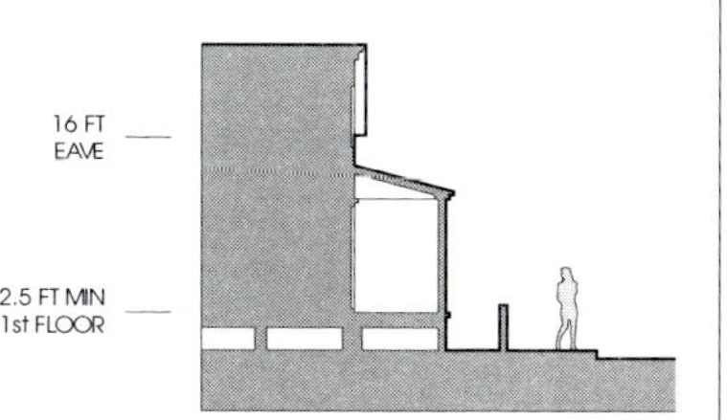

LANDSCAPE REGULATIONS

FRONT YARD

: *MAY BE PLANTED WITH SHRUBS, HEDGES, FLOWERS AND/OR GRASS*
: *LAWN AREA MAY BE 30% MIN OF THE TOTAL LOT AREA*
: *VINES MAY BE PLANTED TO GROW ON PORCHES*

PERIMETER

: A CONTINUOUS HEDGE IS REQUIRED AT A MINIMUM OF 6 FT HEIGHT AT THE SIDES & REAR
: DEPENDING ON THE STREET TYPE, THE FRONT ELEVATION MAY BE SCREENED WITH TREES AND PALMS

DRIVEWAY

: MAY BE PLANTED WITH SHRUBS, HEDGES, FLOWERS AND/OR GRASS
: 12 FT MAX WIDTH
: SHALL BE A STREIGHT PERPENDICULAR PAVED AREA RUNNING FROM THE STREET TO PARKING

RIGHT-OF-WAY

: MAY BE PLANTED WITH PALMS AND TREES
: UNPAVED AREAS SHALL BE PLANTED WITH GRASS

Conch Eyebrow:

This building type is a two-story home with a front porch running parallel to the street, a two room deep footprint plus a central hallway, a comfortable private yard and on-site parking. It presents covered second-story windows and tall columns in the porch. This building is used either as the main structure or as an out-building with the its main structure located in the rear. The building is raised on a pier foundation to allow for air circulation, flooding recharge and privacy.

The common building name is "Classic Revival Eyebrow."

Case Studies:

ADDRESS
: 525 Margaret
: 1025 Flemming
: 1221 Petronia
: 401 Frances

STREET VIEW

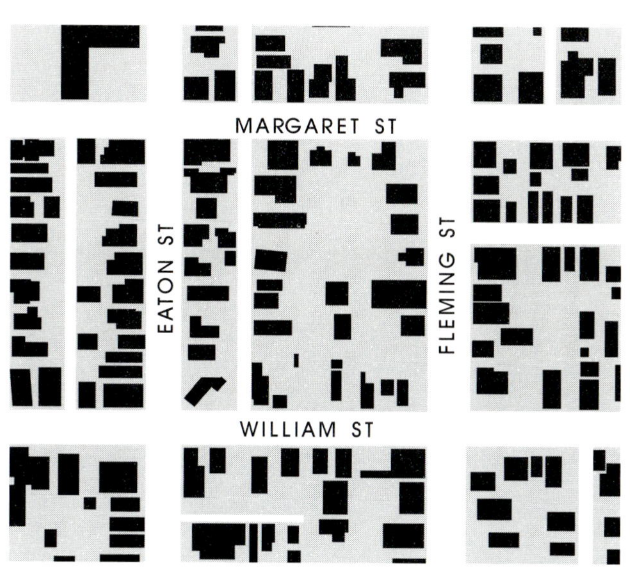

BLOCK

Block Type:

BLOCK	: 400 ft X 450 ft
TOTAL LOTS	: 33
CORNER	: 8 ft radius

Street Type:

SPATIAL RATIO	: 1:3 (Height to Width)
R.O.W.	: 40 ft
LANE(S)	: Two lanes, one way
PARKING	: Parallel, one side
SIDEWALK	: 10 ft one side and 5 ft one side
LANDSCAPE	: Tropical
STREETSCAPE	: Lamp post
SIGNAGE	: Posted on main structure
ELECTRICITY	: Overhead wiring
USE	: Mixed-Use
ORIENTATION	: Southeast

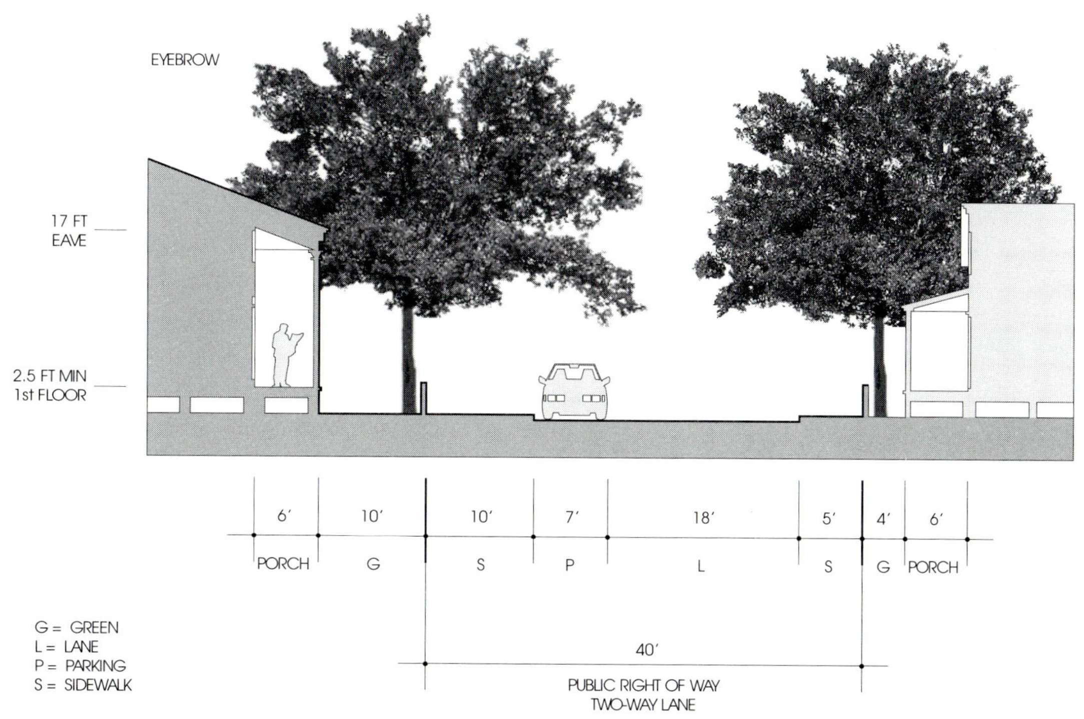

STREET SECTION THROUGH FLEMING STREET

Lot Type:

TYPE	: Rear yard
COVERAGE	: 15 %
F.A.R.	: 30 %
PERVIOUS AREA	: 65 %
SIZE	: 50 ft X 85 ft
PARKING	: Two car parking on site
FRONT YARD	: 16 ft
SIDE YARD	: 4 ft
REAR YARD	: 25 ft
ENCROACHMENT	: 6 ft maximum, with open structure
OUTBUILDING	: None
FENCE	: 4 ft high front and 6 ft high sides and rear
DRIVEWAY	: Wdth 18 ft maximum, perpendicular to street

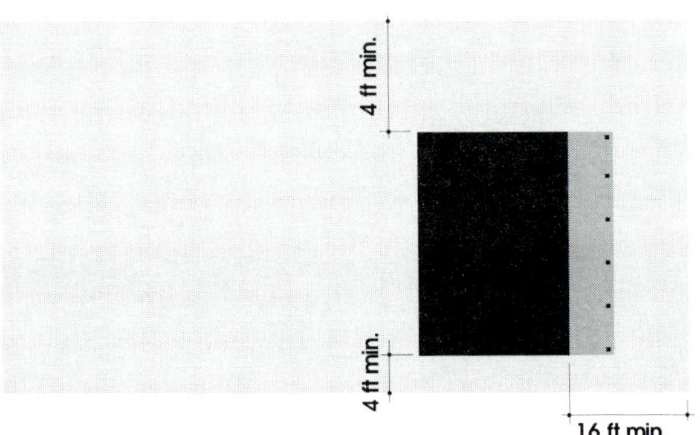

BUILDING LOT

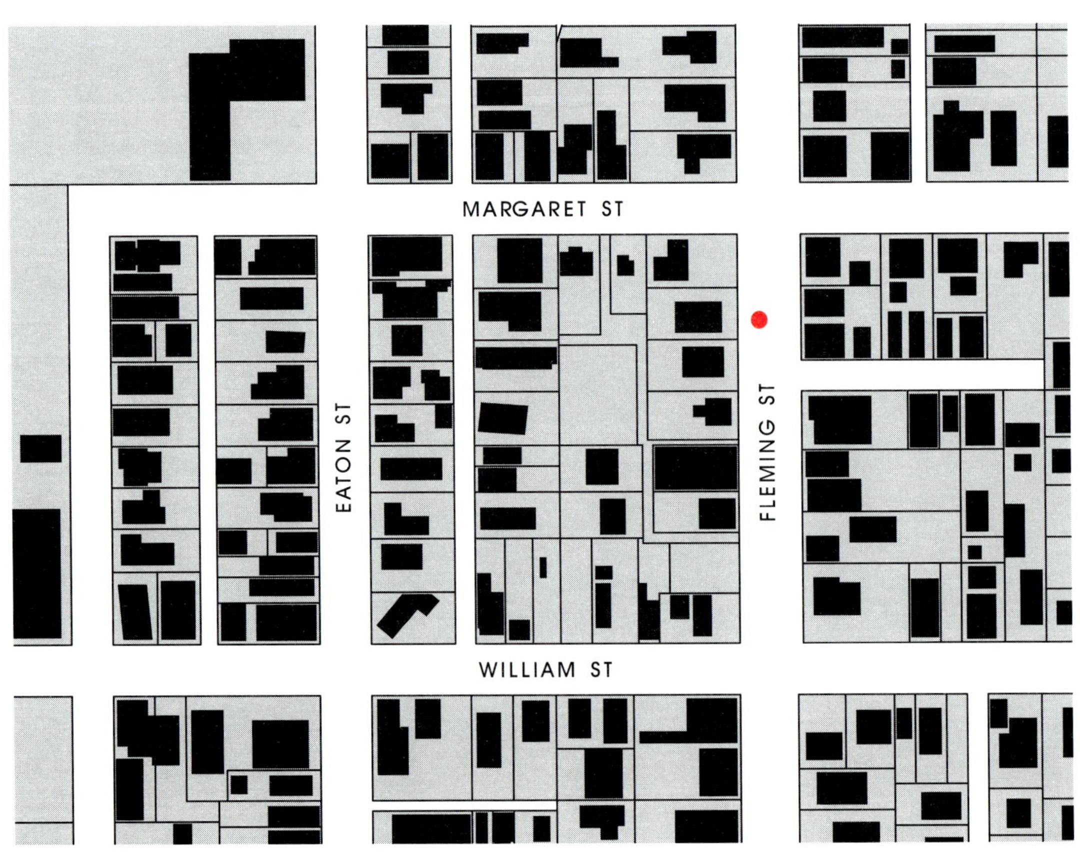

LOCATION MAP

FRONT ELEVATION

BUILDING TYPE:

CONSTRUCTION	: Wood frame
USE	: Residential
UNITS/ACRE	: 6.5
FACADE ASPECT	: Porch
PORCH	: 6 ft
CLIMATE CONTROL	: Porch for screening the sun, air vents and double hung windows for natural ventilation
SECURITY	: Public rooms and main entrance off the sidewalk
WINDOW/DOOR	: Vertical proportions

BUILDING FINISH:

WALLS	: Wood siding
ROOF	: Galvanized metal
COLOR	: White and green shutters
PRIVACY	: Fences, raised floor and land-scaping

PEDESTRIAN VIEW

PLAN TYPE:

CHARACTERISTIC	: Central hall
SHAPE	: Rectangular
FOOTPRINT	: 30 ft X 20 ft
SQUARE FOOTAGE	: 1200 to 1500 sq ft
FIRST LEVEL	: 2.5 ft above the sidewalk
ORIENTATION	: Parallel to main street
KITCHEN	: 1st floor, overlooking garden
DINING ROOM	: 1st floor, overlooking sidewalk
LIVING ROOM	: 1st floor, overlooking sidewalk
SLEEPING ROOM	: 2nd floor
YARD	: Semi-public front, private rear
OUTBUILDING	: None

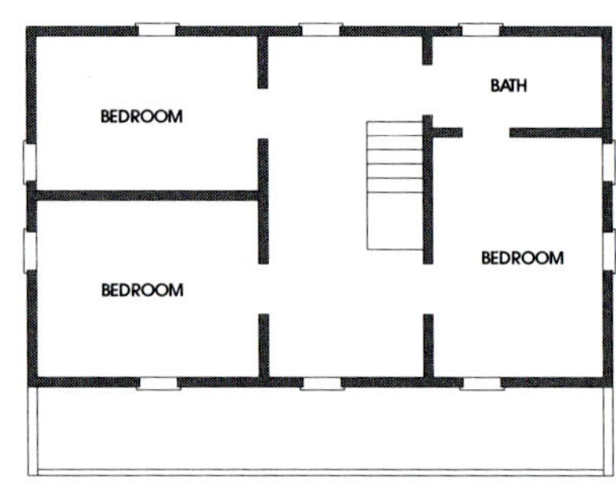

SECOND FLOOR

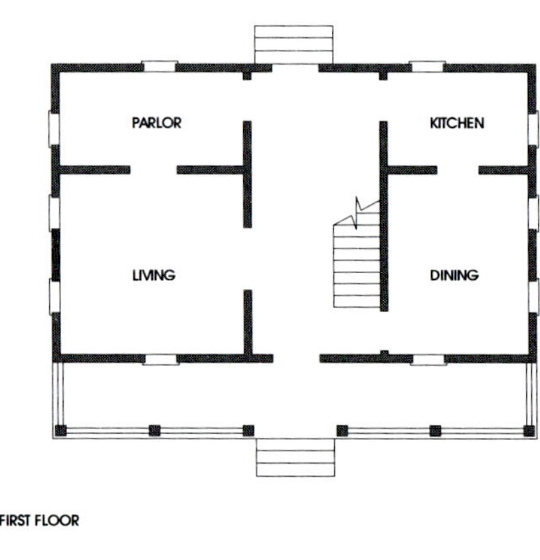

FIRST FLOOR

FLOOR PLANS

THE URBAN AND LANDSCAPE REGULATIONS WERE DERIVED FROM AN ANALYSIS OF SANDBORN MAPS, HISTORIC AMERICAN BUILDING SURVEYS, AERIALS, SITE VISITS, AND CONVERSATIONS WITH LOCAL RESIDENTS, HISTORIC PRESERVATION GROUPS, ARCHITECTS, LANDSCAPE ARCHITECTS, TRAFFIC ENGINEERS, SCHOOLS OF ARCHITECTURE AND PLANNING, AND ZONING DEPARTMENTS.

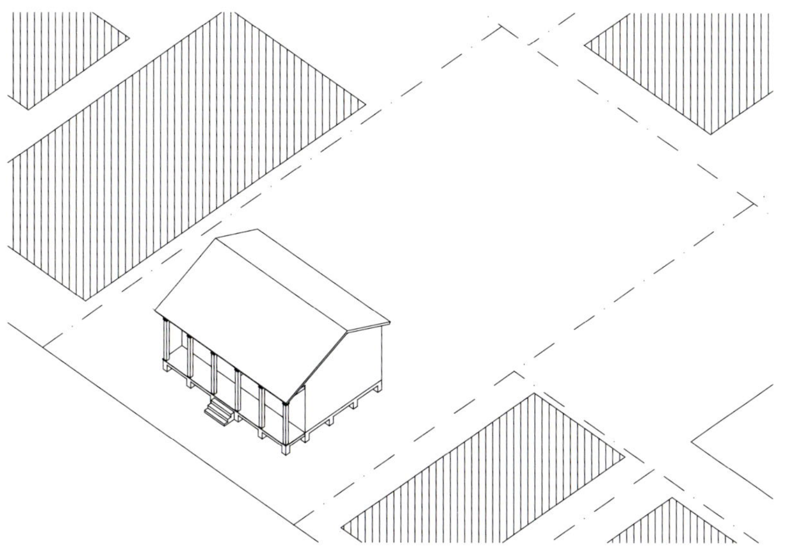

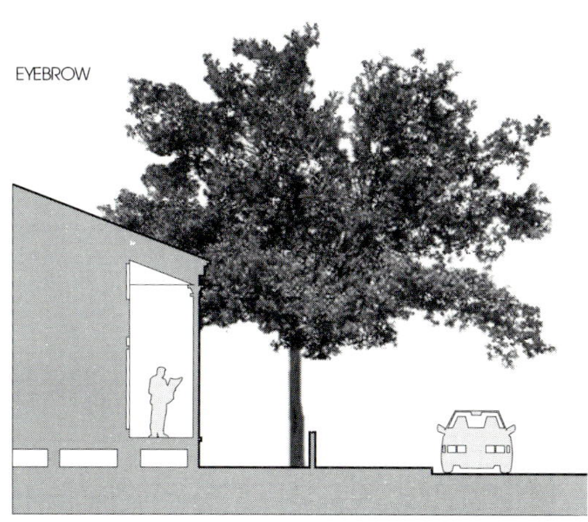

URBAN REGULATIONS

PLACEMENT

: 15 % MAXIMUM BUILDING LOT COVERAGE
: 65 % MINIMUM PERVIOUS AREA
: 65 % MINIMUM STREET FRONTAGE BUILD-OUT
: 16 FT MINIMUM FRONT YARD
: 4 FT MINIMUM SIDE STREET YARD
: 25 FT MINIMUM REAR YARD

FRONT

ENCROACHMENT

: 6 FT MINIMUM DEPTH FRONT PORCH REQUIRED AND 100% MINIMUM WIDTH

PARKING / OUTBUILDING

: TWO CAR SPACE ALLOWED
: 20 FT X 20 FT MAXIMUM
: 4 FT MINIMUM SIDE YARD SETBACKS

HEIGHT & USE

: 17 FT MAXIMUM BUILDING EAVE
: FIRST FLOOR RESIDENTIAL
: SECOND FLOOR RESIDENTIAL

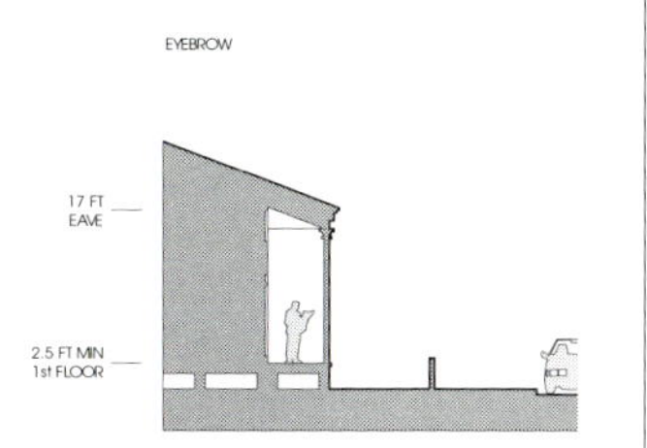

LANDSCAPE REGULATIONS

FRONT YARD

: *MAY BE PLANTED WITH SHRUBS, HEDGES, FLOWERS AND/OR GRASS*
: *LAWN AREA 30% MINIMUM OF THE TOTAL LOT AREA*
: *VINES MAY BE PLANTED TO GROW ON PORCHES*

PERIMETER

: A CONTINUOUS HEDGE IS REQUIRED AT A MINIMUM OF 6 FT HEIGHT AT THE SIDES & REAR
: DEPENDING ON THE STREET TYPE, THE FRONT ELEVATION MAY BE SCREENED WITH TREES AND PALMS

DRIVEWAY

: MAY BE PLANTED WITH SHRUBS, HEDGES, FLOWERS AND/OR GRASS
: 20 FT MAXIMUM WIDTH
: SHALL BE A STRAIGHT, PERPENDICULAR PAVED AREA RUNNING FROM THE STREET TO PARKING

RIGHT-OF-WAY

: MAY BE PLANTED WITH PALMS AND TREES
: UNPAVED AREAS SHALL BE PLANTED WITH GRASS

Conch Cottage:

This building type is a single family home with a front porch that runs parallel to the street; it has a small footprint (two-room wide plus hallway), a comfortable private yard, and on-site parking. The plan is organized around a central hall running along the entire depth of the building. The building is raised on a pier foundation to allow for air circulation, flooding recharge and privacy. It is placed back from the sidewalk to allow for a semi-private front yard.

The common building name is "Classic Revival Cottage."

Case Study:

ADDRESS : 311 William Street

STREET VIEW

MARGARET ST
CAROLINE ST
EATON ST
WILLIAM ST

BLOCK

Block Type:

BLOCK	: 450 ft X 400 ft
TOTAL LOTS	: 43
CORNER	: 8 ft radius

Street Type:

SPATIAL RATIO	: 1:3 (Height to Width)
R.O.W.	: 50 ft
LANE(S)	: Two lanes both directions
PARKING	: Parallel, one side
SIDEWALK	: 10 ft, both sides
LANDSCAPE	: Tropical
STREETSCAPE	: Lamp post
SIGNAGE	: Posted on main structure
ELECTRICITY	: Overhead wiring
USE	: Mixed-Use
ORIENTATION	: Southeast

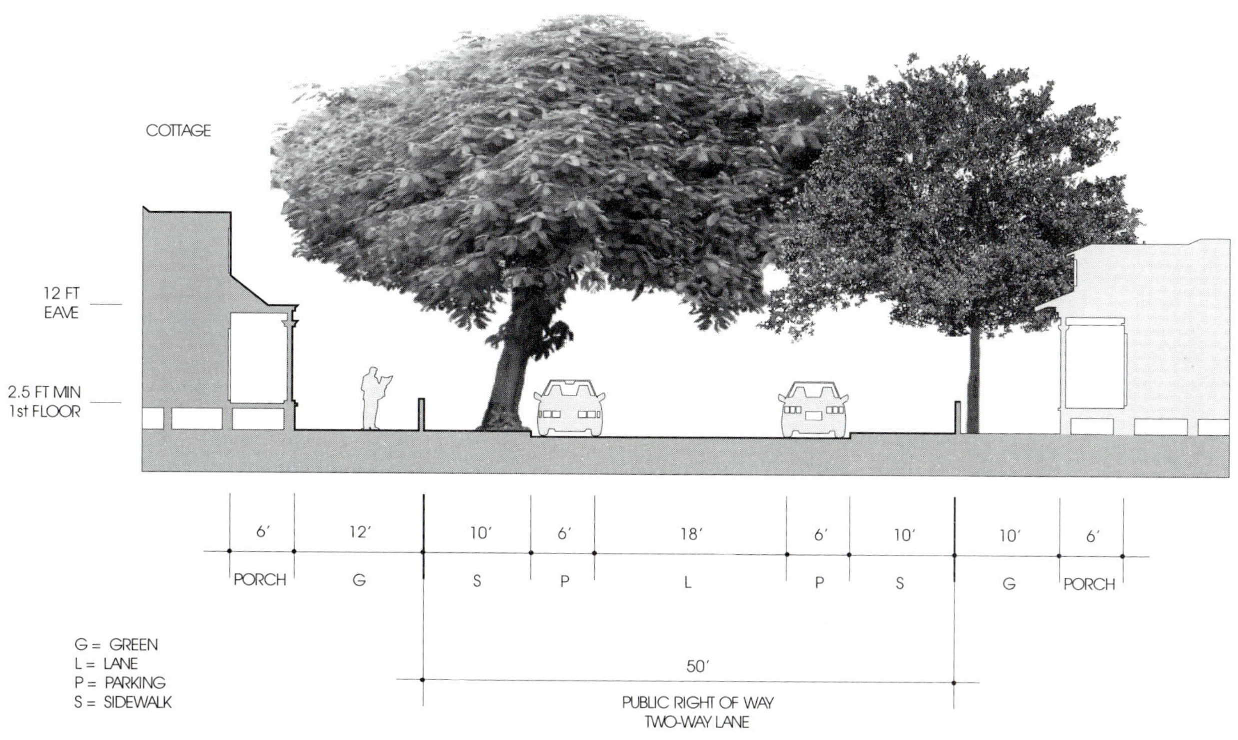

STREET SECTION THROUGH WILLIAM STREET

LOT TYPE:

TYPE	: Rear yard
COVERAGE	: 20 %
F.A.R.	: 40 %
PERVIOUS AREA	: 65 %
SIZE	: 55 ft X 95 ft
PARKING	: Two car parking on site
FRONT YARD	: 12 ft
SIDE YARD	: 12 ft
REAR YARD	: 30 ft
ENCROACHMENT	: 6 ft maximum, with open structure
OUTBUILDING	: Attached to main structure
FENCE	: 4 ft high front and 6 ft high sides and rear
DRIVEWAY	: Width 18 ft maximum, perpendicular to street

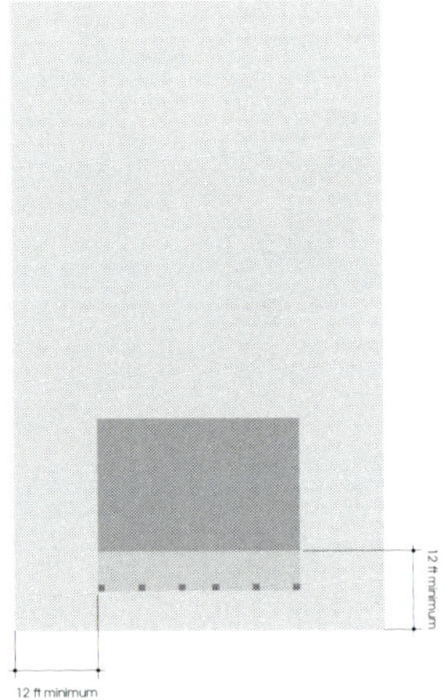

BUILDING LOT

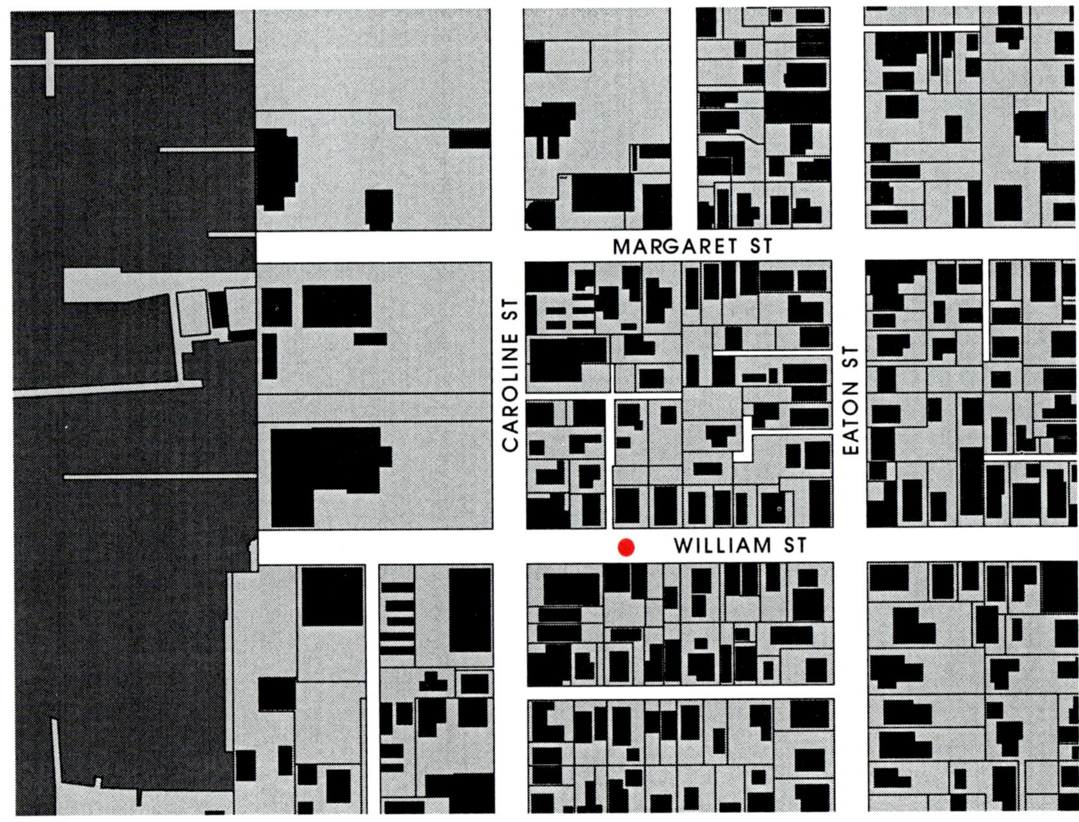

LOCATION MAP

FRONT ELEVATION

BUILDING TYPE:

CONSTRUCTION	: Wood frame
USE	: Residential
UNITS/ACRE	: 8
FACADE ASPECT	: Porch
PORCH	: 6 ft
CLIMATE CONTROL	: Deep porch for screening the sun, air vents and double hung windows for natural ventilation
SECURITY	: Public rooms and main entrance off the sidewalk
WINDOW/DOOR	: Vertical proportions

BUILDING FINISH:

WALLS	: Wood horizontal siding
ROOF	: Metal shingles or V-crimp metal
COLOR	: White, light gray or pastel shades
PRIVACY	: Fences, raised floor and landscaping

PEDESTRIAN VIEW

PLAN TYPE:

CHARACTERISTIC	: Central hall
SHAPE	: Rectangular
FOOTPRINT	: 35 ft X 20 ft
SQUARE FOOTAGE	: 1200 to 1500 sq ft
FIRST LEVEL	: 2.5 ft above the sidewalk
ORIENTATION	: Perpendicular to the main street
KITCHEN	: 1st floor, overlooking rear yard
DINING ROOM	: 1st floor, overlooking rear yard
LIVING ROOM	: 1st floor, overlooking sidewalk
BEDROOM(S)	: 1st & 2nd floors
YARD	: Semi-public front, private rear
OUTBUILDING	: None

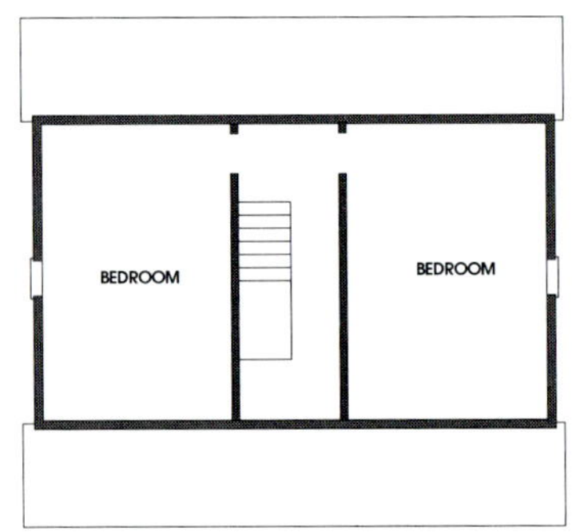

SECOND FLOOR PLAN

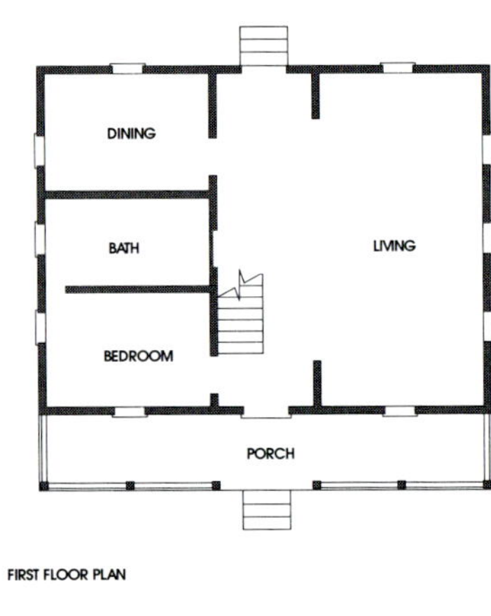

FIRST FLOOR PLAN

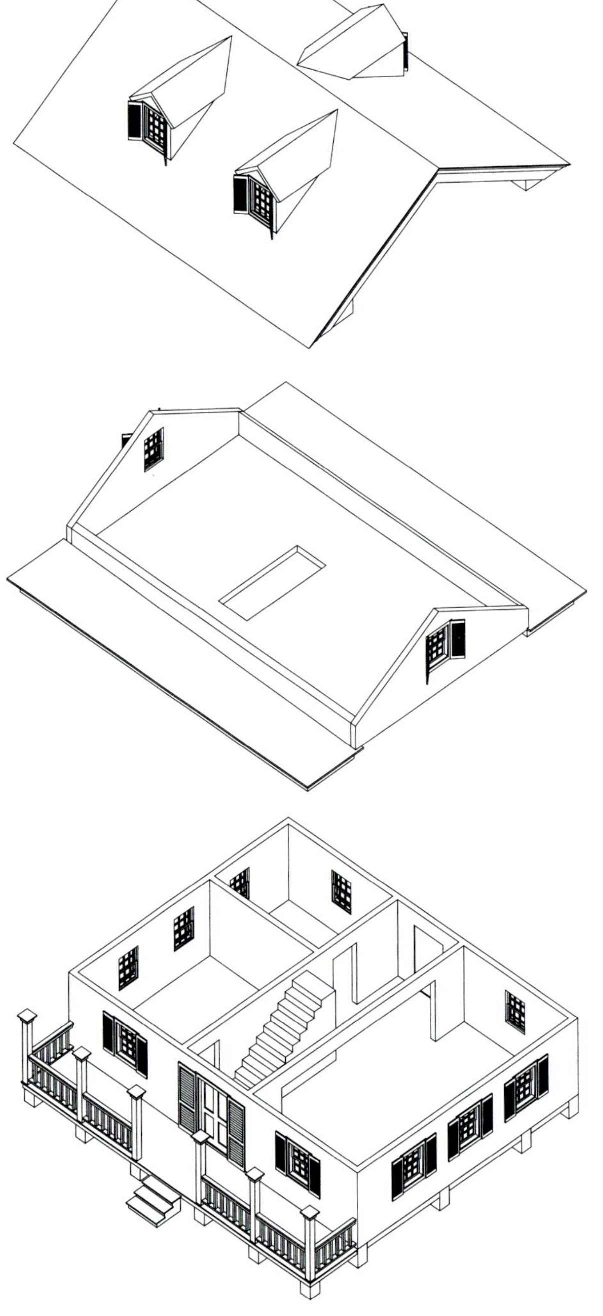

FLOOR PLANS

THE URBAN AND LANDSCAPE REGULATIONS WERE DERIVED FROM AN ANALYSIS OF SANDBORN MAPS, HISTORIC AMERICAN BUILDING SURVEYS, AERIALS, SITE VISITS, AND CONVERSATIONS WITH LOCAL RESIDENTS, HISTORIC PRESERVATION GROUPS, ARCHITECTS, LANDSCAPE ARCHITECTS, TRAFFIC ENGINEERS, SCHOOLS OF ARCHITECTURE AND PLANNING, AND ZONING DEPARTMENTS.

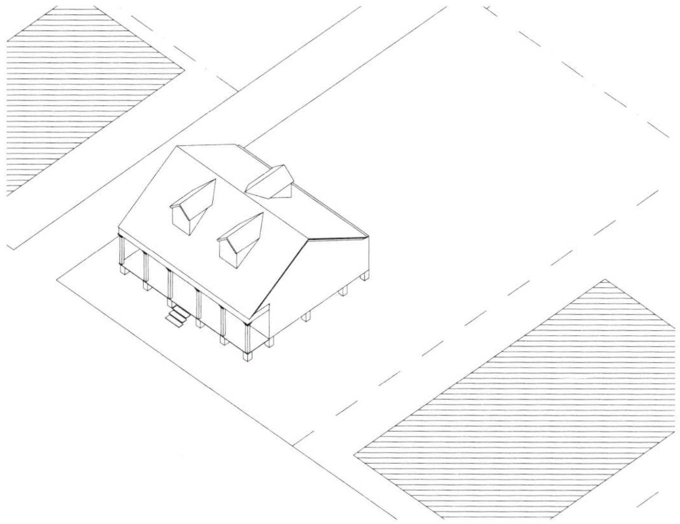

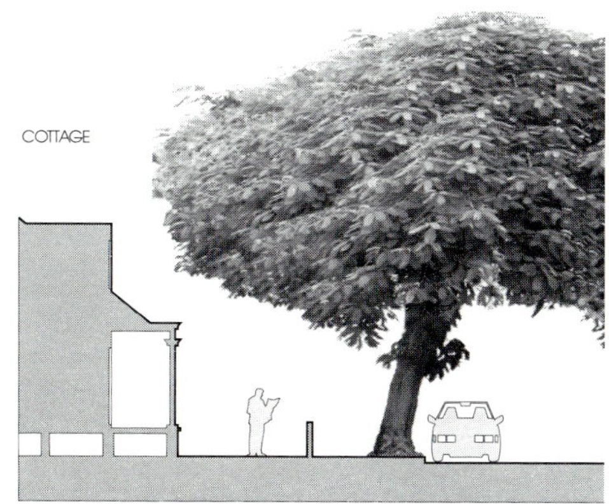

URBAN REGULATIONS

PLACEMENT

: 20 % MAXIMUM BUILDING LOT COVERAGE
: 65 % MINIMUM PERVIOUS AREA
: 70 % MINIMUM STREET FRONTAGE BUILD-OUT
: 12 FT MINIMUM FRONT YARD
: 12 FT MINIMUM SIDE YARD
: 30 FT MINIMUM REAR YARD

ENCROACHMENT

: 6 FT MINIMUM DEPTH FRONT PORCH REQUIRED AND 100 % MINIMUM WIDTH

PARKING / OUTBUILDING

: TWO CAR SPACE ALLOWED
: 20 FT X 20 FT MAXIMUM
: 2 FT MINIMUM REAR YARD, OUTBUILDING
: 5 FT MINIMUM SIDE YARD, PARKING

HEIGHT & USE

: 12 FT MAXIMUM BUILDING EAVE
: FIRST FLOOR RESIDENTIAL
: SECOND FLOOR RESIDENTIAL

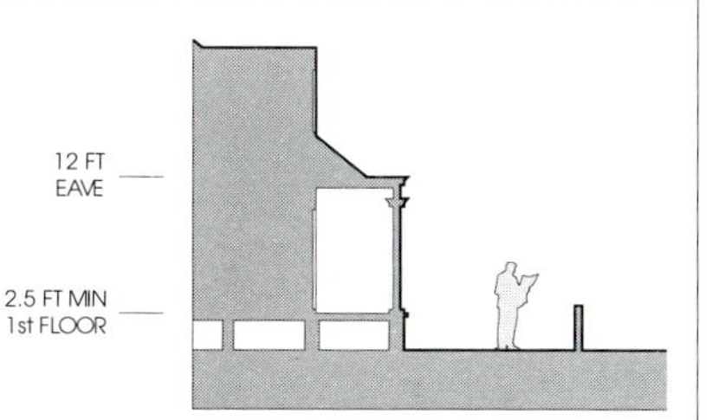

LANDSCAPE REGULATIONS

FRONT YARD

: *MAY BE PLANTED WITH SHRUBS, HEDGES, FLOWERS AND/OR GRASS*
: *LAWN AREA MAY BE 30% MINIMUM OF THE TOTAL LOT AREA*
: *VINES MAY BE PLANTED TO GROW ON PORCHES*

PERIMETER

: A CONTINUOUS HEDGE IS REQUIRED AT A MINIMUM OF 6 FT HEIGHT AT THE SIDES & REAR
: DEPENDING ON THE STREET TYPE, THE FRONT ELEVATION MAY BE SCREENED WITH TREES AND PALMS

DRIVEWAY

: MAY BE PLANTED WITH SHRUBS, HEDGES, FLOWERS AND/OR GRASS
: 18 FT MAXIMUM WIDTH
: SHALL BE A STRAIGHT, PERPENDICULAR PAVED AREA RUNNING FROM THE STREET TO PARKING

RIGHT-OF-WAY

: MAY BE PLANTED WITH PALMS AND TREES
: UNPAVED AREAS SHALL BE PLANTED WITH GRASS

CONCH CAPTAIN:

This building type is a single family two story with a front porch parallel to the street, a footprint two rooms wide plus a central hallway, a comfortable private rear yard, and a side yard for on-site parking. The plan is organized around a central hall . The building is raised substantially on a pier foundation to allow for air circulation, flooding recharge and privacy.

The common building name is "Oldest House in Key West."

CASE STUDY:

ADDRESS : 332 Duval Street

STREET VIEW

DUVAL ST
CAROLINE ST
EATON ST
WHITEHEAD ST

BLOCK

Block Type:

BLOCK	: 460 ft X 380 ft
TOTAL LOTS	: 25
CORNER	: 8 ft radius

Street Type:

SPATIAL RATIO	: 1:3 (Height to Width)
R.O.W.	: 50 ft
LANE(S)	: Two lanes, two way
PARKING	: Parallel, one side
SIDEWALK	: 10 ft, both sides
LANDSCAPE	: Tropical
STREETSCAPE	: Lamp post, benches and meters
SIGNAGE	: Posted on main structure
ELECTRICITY	: Overhead wiring
USE	: Mixed-Use
ORIENTATION	: Southeast

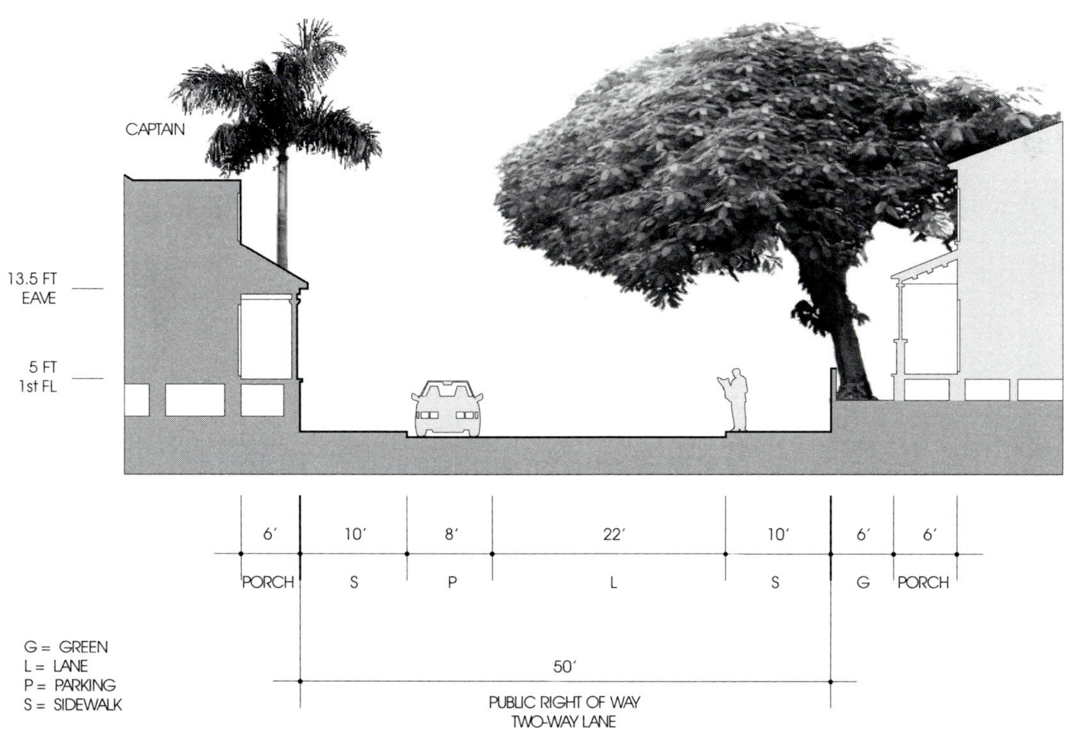

STREET SECTION THROUGH DUVAL STREET

Lot Type:

TYPE	: Rear yard
COVERAGE	: 5 %
F.A.R.	: 10 %
PERVIOUS AREA	: 50 %
SIZE	: 85 ft X 195 ft
PARKING	: Two car parking on site.
FRONT YARD	: 6 ft
SIDE YARD	: 10 ft
REAR YARD	: 115 ft
ENCROACHMENT	: 6 ft maximum, with open structure
OUTBUILDING	: None
FENCE	: 4 ft high front and 6 ft high sides and rear
DRIVEWAY	: Width 10 ft maximum, perpendicular to street

BUILDING LOT

LOCATION MAP

FRONT ELEVATION

Building Type:

CONSTRUCTION	: Wood frame
USE	: Residential
UNITS/ACRE	: 2.8
FACADE ASPECT	: Porch
PORCH	: 6 ft
CLIMATE CONTROL	: Deep porch for screening the sun, air vents and double hung windows for natural ventilation
SECURITY	: Public rooms and main entrance off the sidewalk
WINDOW/DOOR	: Vertical proportions

Building Finish:

WALLS	: Wood siding
ROOF	: Metal shingles or V-crimp
COLOR	: White, light gray or pastel shades
PRIVACY	: Fences, raised floor and landscaping

PEDESTRIAN VIEW

PLAN TYPE:

CHARACTERISTIC	: Central hall
SHAPE	: Rectangular
FOOTPRINT	: 40 ft X 20 ft
SQUARE FOOTAGE	: 1600 to 1800 sq ft
FIRST LEVEL	: 4.5 ft above the sidewalk
ORIENTATION	: Parallel to main street
KITCHEN	: 1st floor, overlooking rear yard
DINING ROOM	: 1st floor, overlooking sidewalk
LIVING ROOM	: 1st floor, overlooking sidewalk
BEDROOM(S)	: 2nd floor
YARD	: Semi-public front, private rear
OUTBUILDING	: None

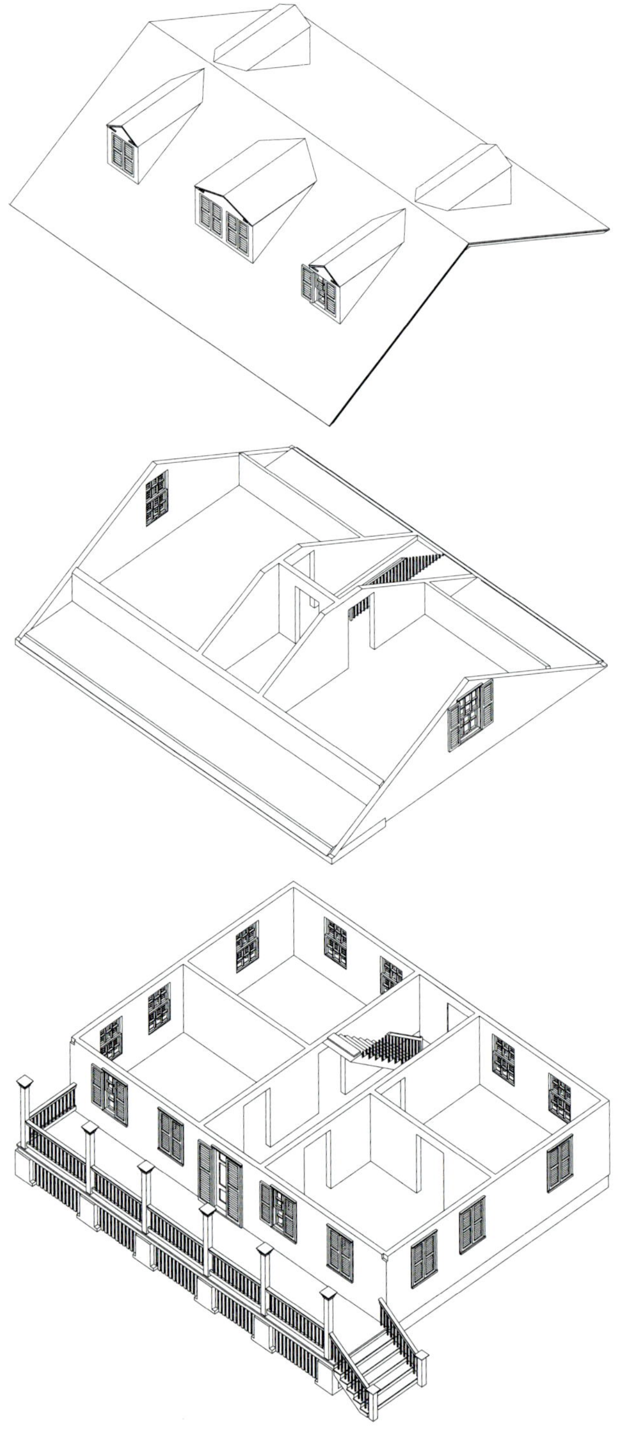

SECOND FLOOR PLAN

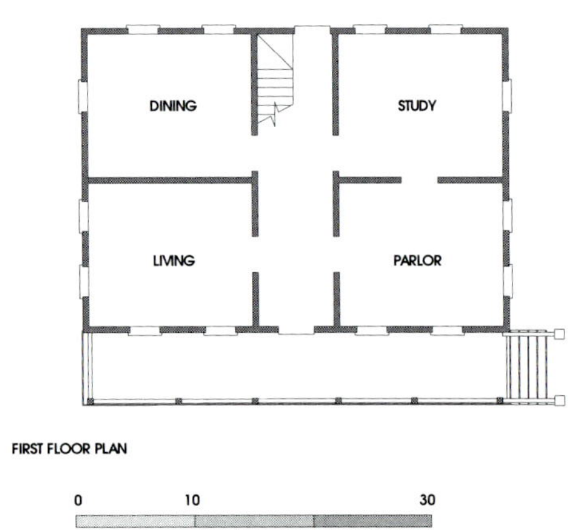

FIRST FLOOR PLAN

0 10 30

FLOOR PLANS

THE URBAN AND LANDSCAPE REGULATIONS WERE DERIVED FROM AN ANALYSIS OF SANDBORN MAPS, HISTORIC AMERICAN BUILDING SURVEYS, AERIALS, SITE VISITS, AND CONVERSATIONS WITH LOCAL RESIDENTS, HISTORIC PRESERVATION GROUPS, ARCHITECTS, LANDSCAPE ARCHITECTS, TRAFFIC ENGINEERS, SCHOOLS OF ARCHITECTURE AND PLANNING, AND ZONING DEPARTMENTS.

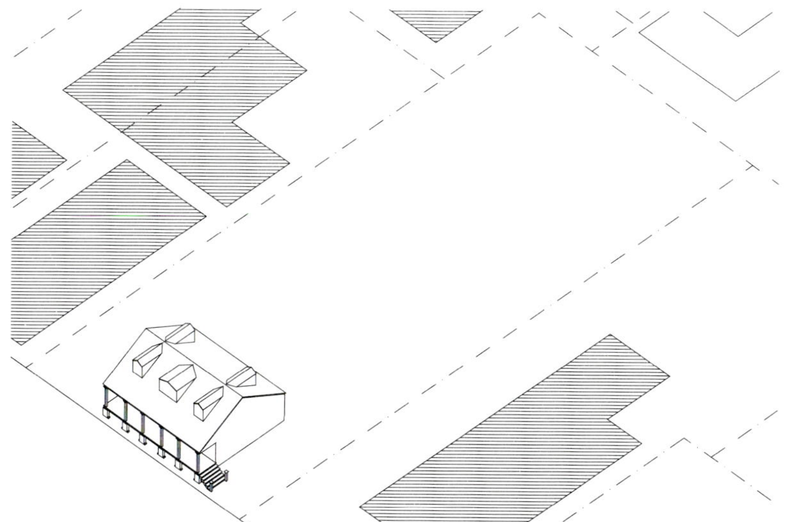

URBAN REGULATIONS

PLACEMENT

FRONT

: 10 % MAXIMUM BUILDING LOT COVERAGE
: 65% MINIMUM PERVIOUS AREA
: 50 % MINIMUM STREET FRONTAGE BUILD-OUT
: 6 FT MINIMUM FRONT YARD
: 10 FT MINIMUM SIDE YARD
: 115 FT MINIMUM REAR YARD

ENCROACHMENT

: 6 FT MINIMUM DEPTH FRONT PORCH REQUIRED AND 100% MINIMUM WIDTH

PARKING / OUTBUILDING

: TWO CAR SPACE ALLOWED
: 20 FT X 20 FT MAXIMUM
: 10 FT MINIMUM SIDE YARD
: NO OUTBUILDING

HEIGHT & USE

: 13.5 FT MAXIMUM BUILDING EAVE
: FIRST FLOOR COMMERCIAL OR RESIDENTIAL
: SECOND FLOOR AND ABOVE RESIDENTIAL

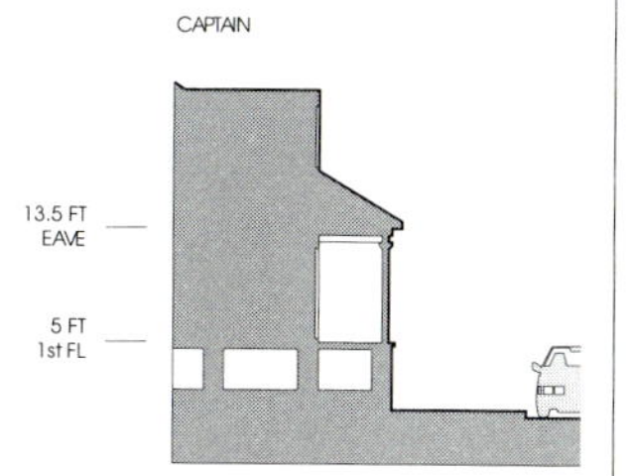

LANDSCAPE REGULATIONS

FRONT YARD

: *MAY BE PLANTED WITH SHRUBS, HEDGES, FLOWERS AND/OR GRASS*
: *LAWN AREA 30% MINIMUM OF THE TOTAL LOT AREA*
: *VINES MAY BE PLANTED TO GROW ON PORCHES*

PERIMETER

: A CONTINUOUS HEDGE IS REQUIRED AT A MINIMUM OF 6 FT HEIGHT AT THE SIDES & REAR
: DEPENDING ON THE STREET TYPE, THE FRONT ELEVATION MAY BE SCREENED WITH TREES AND PALMS

DRIVEWAY

: MAY BE PLANTED WITH SHRUBS, HEDGES, FLOWERS AND/OR GRASS
: 20 FT MAXIMUM IN WIDTH
: SHALL BE A STRAIGHT, PERPENDICULAR PAVED AREA RUNNING FROM THE STREET TO PARKING

RIGHT-OF-WAY

: MAY BE PLANTED WITH PALMS AND TREES
: UNPAVED AREAS SHALL BE PLANTED WITH GRASS

Conch Temple:

This single family two story home has a front porch running perpendicular to the street, a one room wide plus a side hallway, a comfortable private rear yard and on-site parking. The plan is articulated along the side hall. The building is raised on a pier foundation to allow for air circulation, flooding recharge and privacy.

The common building name is "Classic Revival Three Bay, Two Story or Classic Revival Temple."

Case Studies:

ADDRESS	: 804 Caroline
	: 409 William
	: 626 William
	: 610 White

STREET VIEW

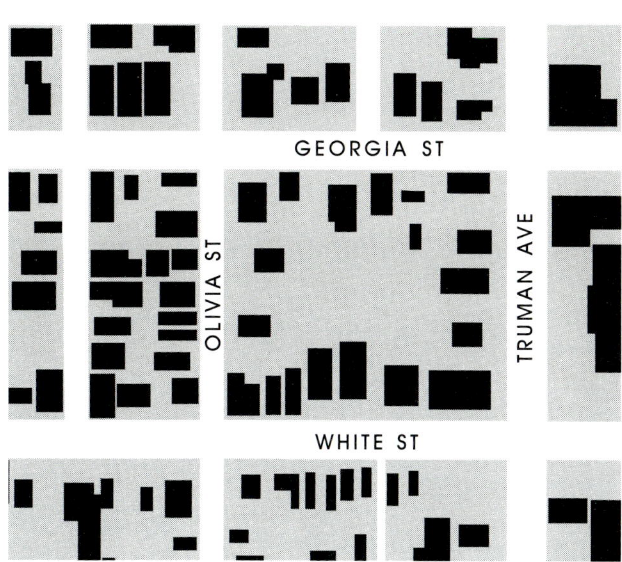

BLOCK

Block Type:

BLOCK	: 360 ft X 320 ft
TOTAL LOTS	: 20
CORNER	: 8 ft radius

Street Type:

SPATIAL RATIO	: 1:3 (Height to Width)
R.O.W.	: 50 ft
LANE(S)	: Two lanes, two way
PARKING	: Parallel, two sides
SIDEWALK	: 10 ft, both sides
LANDSCAPE	: Tropical
STREETSCAPE	: Lamp post
SIGNAGE	: Posted on main structure
ELECTRICITY	: Overhead wiring
USE	: Mixed-Use
ORIENTATION	: Southeast

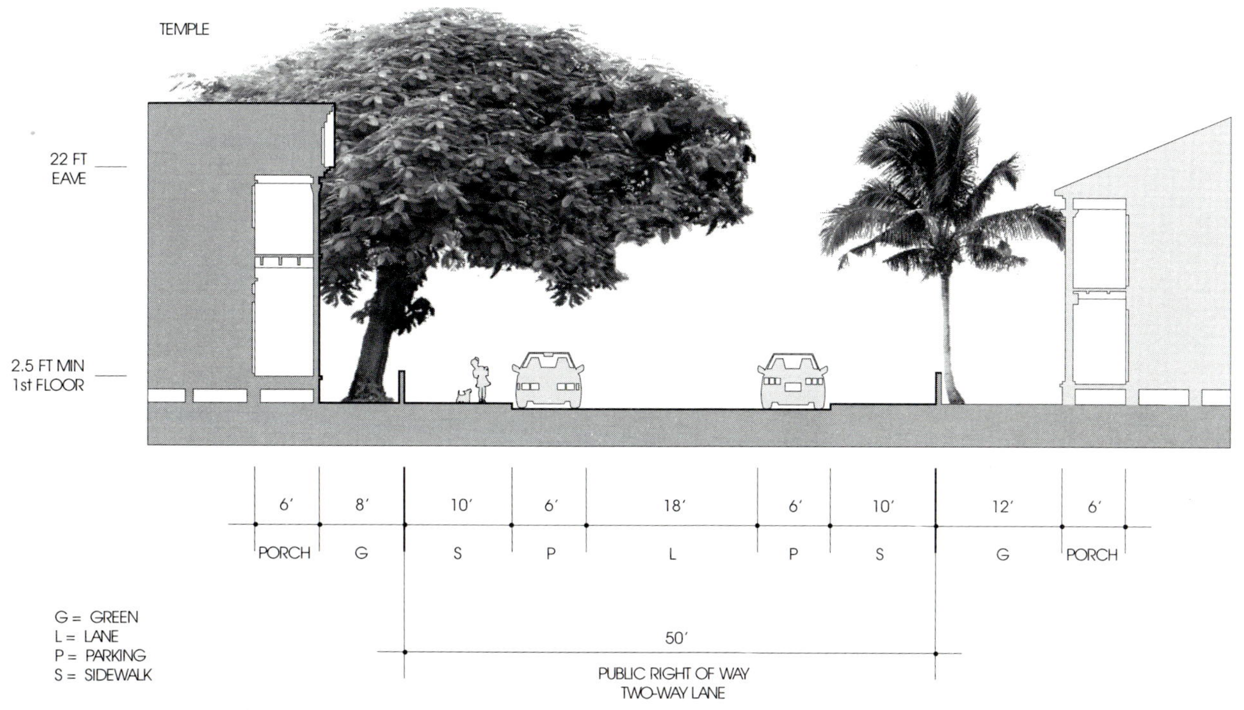

STREET SECTION THROUGH GEORGIA STREET

Lot Type:

TYPE	: Rear yard
COVERAGE	: 50 %
F.A.R.	: 40 %
PERVIOUS AREA	: 30 %
SIZE	: 40 ft X 120 ft
PARKING	: Two car parking on site
FRONT YARD	: 15 ft
SIDE YARD	: 5 ft
REAR YARD	: 15 ft
ENCROACHMENT	: 6 ft maximum, with open structure
OUTBUILDING	: None
FENCE	: 4 ft high front and 6 ft high sides and rear
DRIVEWAY	: Width 12' maximum, perpendicular to street

BUILDING LOT

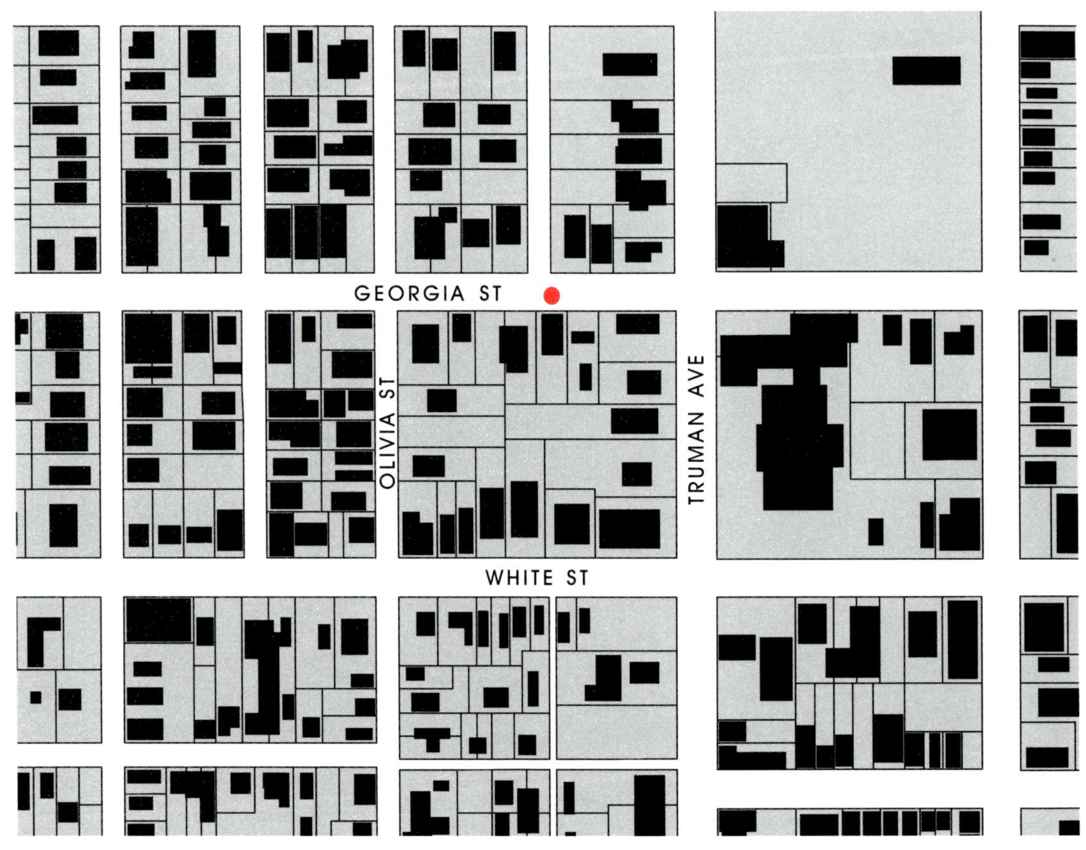

LOCATION MAP

FRONT ELEVATION

BUILDING TYPE:

CONSTRUCTION	: Wood frame
USE	: Residential
UNITS/ACRE	: 9
FACADE ASPECT	: Porch
PORCH	: 6 ft
CLIMATE CONTROL	: Deep porch for screening the sun, air vents and double hung windows for natural ventilation
SECURITY	: Public rooms and main entrance off the sidewalk
WINDOW/DOOR	: Vertical proportions

BUILDING FINISH:

WALLS	: Wood siding
ROOF	: Metal shingles or V-crimp
COLOR	: White, light gray or pastel shades
PRIVACY	: Fences, raised floor and landscaping

PEDESTRIAN VIEW

PLAN TYPE:

CHARACTERISTIC	: Central hall
SHAPE	: Rectangular
FOOTPRINT	: 24 ft X 40 ft
SQUARE FOOTAGE	: 1400 to 1950 sq ft
FIRST LEVEL	: 2.5 ft above the sidewalk
ORIENTATION	: Perpendicular to main street
KITCHEN	: 1st floor, overlooking rear yard
DINING ROOM	: 1st floor, overlooking rear yard
LIVING ROOM	: 1st floor, overlooking sidewalk
BEDROOM(S)	: 2nd & 3rd floors
YARD	: Semi-public front, private rear
OUTBUILDING	: None

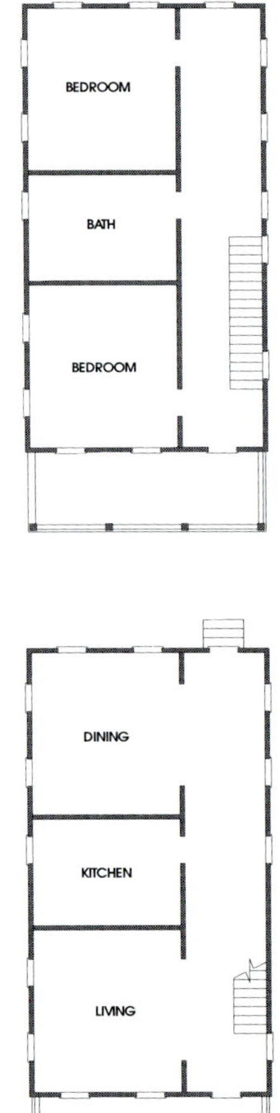

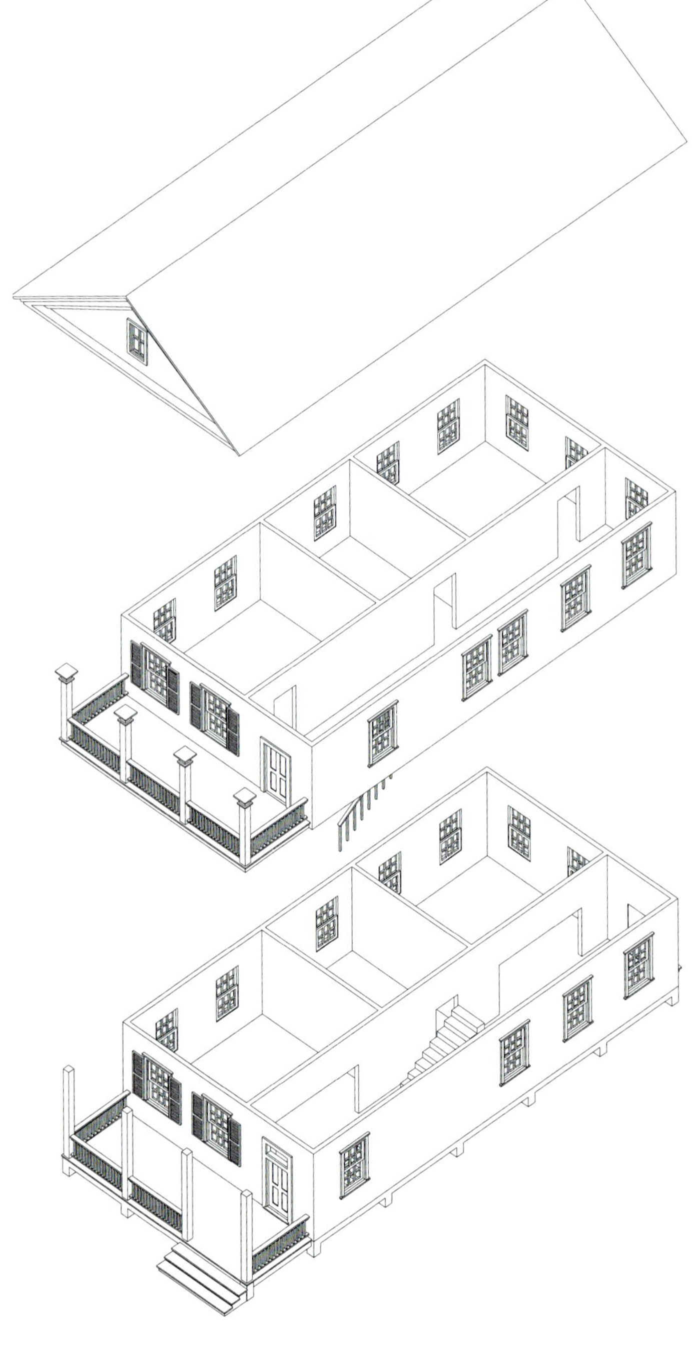

TYPICAL FLOOR PLAN

THE URBAN AND LANDSCAPE REGULATIONS WERE DERIVED FROM AN ANALYSIS OF SANDBORN MAPS, HISTORIC AMERICAN BUILDING SURVEYS, AERIALS, SITE VISITS, AND CONVERSATIONS WITH LOCAL RESIDENTS, HISTORIC PRESERVATION GROUPS, ARCHITECTS, LANDSCAPE ARCHITECTS, TRAFFIC ENGINEERS, SCHOOLS OF ARCHITECTURE AND PLANNING AND ZONING DEPARTMENTS.

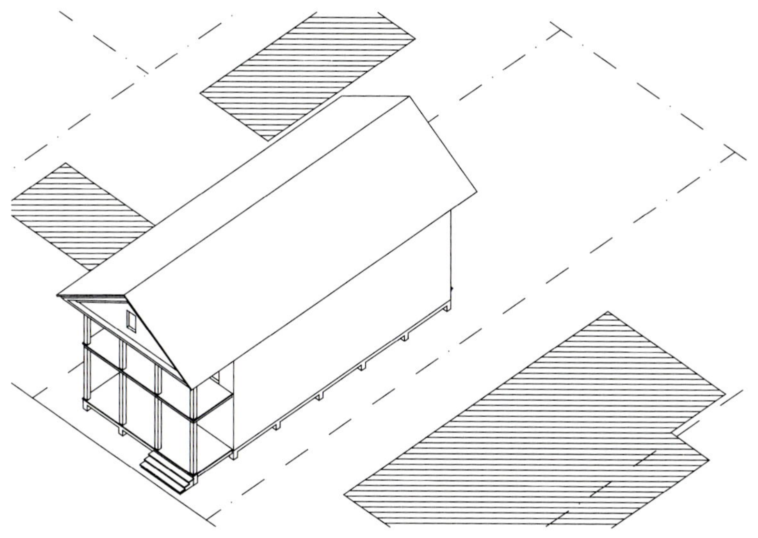

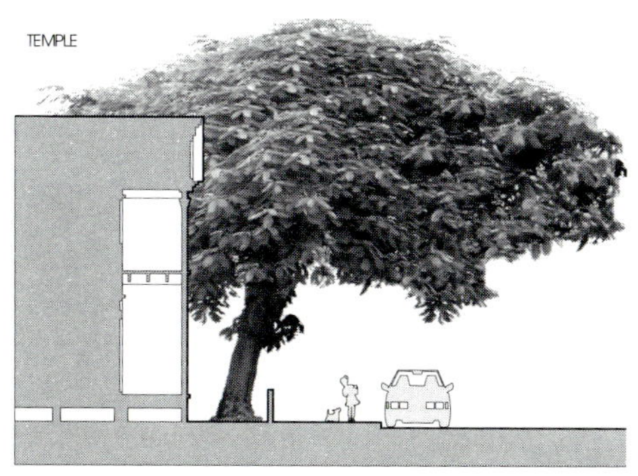

URBAN REGULATIONS

PLACEMENT

FRONT

: 50 % MAXIMUM BUILDING LOT COVERAGE
: 65% MINIMUM PERVIOUS AREA
: 65 % MINIMUM STREET FRONTAGE BUILD-OUT
: 15 FT MINIMUM FRONT YARD
: 5 FT MINIMUM SIDE YARD
: 15 FT MINIMUM REAR YARD

ENCROACHMENT

: 6 FT MINIMUM DEPTH FRONT PORCH REQUIRED AND 90% MINIMUM WIDTH
: 3 FT MINIMUM EXTERIOR STAIRS ON INTERIOR YARD

PARKING / OUTBUILDING

: TWO CAR SPACE ALLOWED
: 20 FT X 20 FT MAXIMUM
: 5 FT MINIMUM SIDE YARD

HEIGHT & USE

: 22 FT MAXIMUM BUILDING EAVE
: FIRST FLOOR COMMERCIAL OR RESIDENTIAL
: SECOND FLOOR AND ABOVE RESIDENTIAL

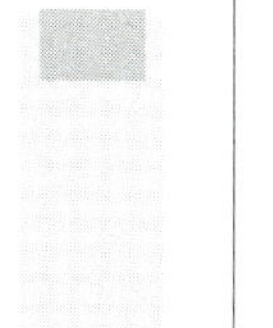

LANDSCAPE REGULATIONS

FRONT YARD

: *MAY BE PLANTED WITH SHRUBS, HEDGES, FLOWERS AND/OR GRASS*
: *LAWN AREA 30% MINIMUM OF THE TOTAL LOT AREA*
: *VINES MAY BE PLANTED TO GROW ON PORCHES*

PERIMETER

: A CONTINUOUS HEDGE IS REQUIRED AT A MINIMUM OF 6 FT HEIGHT AT THE SIDES & REAR
: DEPENDING ON THE STREET TYPE, THE FRONT ELEVATION MAY BE SCREENED WITH TREES AND PALMS

DRIVEWAY

: MAY BE PLANTED WITH SHRUBS, HEDGES, FLOWERS AND/OR GRASS
: 20 FT MAXIMUM WIDTH
: SHALL BE A STRAIGHT, PERPENDICULAR PAVED AREA RUNNING FROM THE STREET TO PARKING

RIGHT-OF-WAY

: MAY BE PLANTED WITH PALMS AND TREES
: UNPAVED AREAS SHALL BE PLANTED WITH GRASS

Conch Four Square:

This single family two story home has a front porch running parallel to the street, a two-room wide footprint plus a central hallway, a comfortable private rear yard, and on-site parking. The plan is organized around a central hallway. The building is raised on a pier foundation to allow for air circulation, flooding recharge and privacy.

The common building name is "Four-Square."

Case Study:

ADDRESS : 617 Angela Street

STREET VIEW

BLOCK

Block Type:

BLOCK	: 415 ft X 400 ft
TOTAL LOTS	: 27
CORNER	: 8 ft radius

Street Type:

SPATIAL RATIO	: 1:3 (Height to Width)
R.O.W.	: 40 ft
LANE(S)	: Two lanes, one way
PARKING	: Parallel, both sides
SIDEWALK	: 6 ft, both sides
LANDSCAPE	: Tropical
STREETSCAPE	: Lamp post
SIGNAGE	: Posted on main structure
ELECTRICITY	: Overhead wiring
USE	: Mixed-Use
ORIENTATION	: Southeast

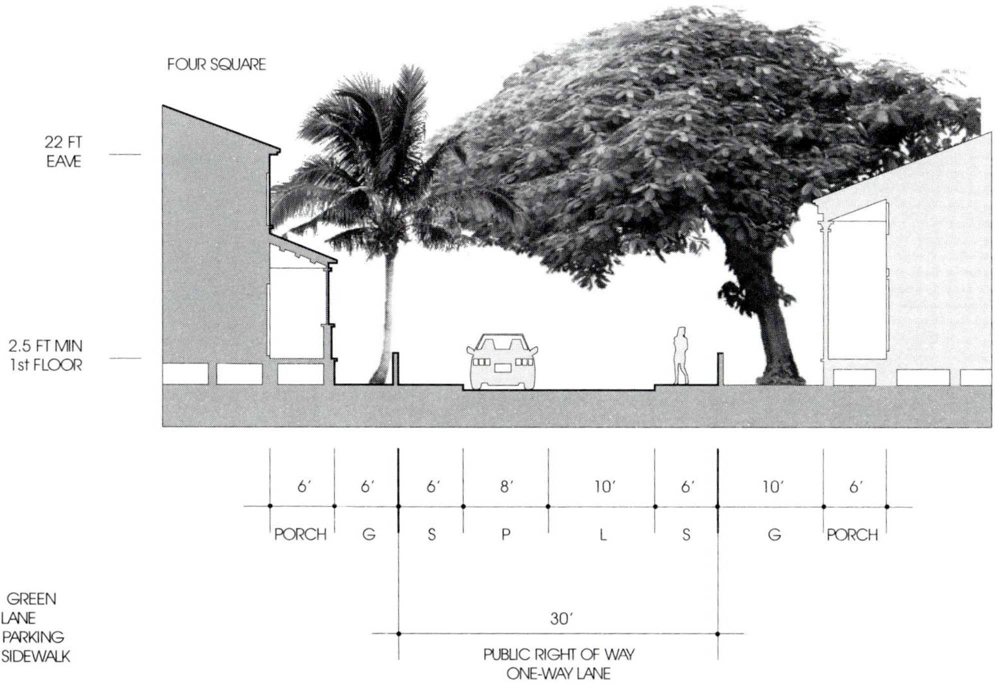

STREET SECTION THROUGH ANGELA STREET

Lot Type:

TYPE	: Rear yard
COVERAGE	: 20 %
F.A.R.	: 40 %
PERVIOUS AREA	: 65 %
SIZE	: 100 ft X 40 ft
PARKING	: Two car parking on site
FRONT YARD	: 15 ft
SIDE YARD	: 6 ft
REAR YARD	: 30 ft
ENCROACHMENT	: 5 ft maximum, with open structure
OUTBUILDING	: In the rear yard
FENCE	: 4 ft high front and 6 ft high sides and rear
DRIVEWAY	: Wdth 12 ft maximum, perpendicular to street

BUILDING LOT

LOCATION MAP

FRONT ELEVATION

Building Type:

CONSTRUCTION	: Wood frame
USE	: Residential
UNITS/ACRE	: 6
FACADE ASPECT	: Porch
PORCH	: 5 ft
CLIMATE CONTROL	: Porch for screening the sun, air vents and double hung windows for natural ventilation
SECURITY	: Public rooms and main entrance off the sidewalk
WINDOW/DOOR	: Vertical proportions

Building Finish:

WALLS	: Wood siding
ROOF	: Metal shingles or V-crimp
COLOR	: White, light grar or pastel shades
PRIVACY	: Fences, raised floor and land-scaping

PEDESTRIAN VIEW

PLAN TYPE:

CHARACTERISTIC	: Central hall
SHAPE	: Square
FOOTPRINT	: 20 ft X 20 ft
SQUARE FOOTAGE	: 800 to 1200 sq ft
FIRST LEVEL	: 2.5 ft above the sidewalk
ORIENTATION	: Parallel to main street
KITCHEN	: 1st floor, overlooking rear yard
DINING ROOM	: 1st floor, overlooking sidewalk
LIVING ROOM	: 1st floor, overlooking sidewalk
BEDROOM(S)	: 2nd floor
YARD	: Semi-public front, private rear
OUTBUILDING	: In the rear yard

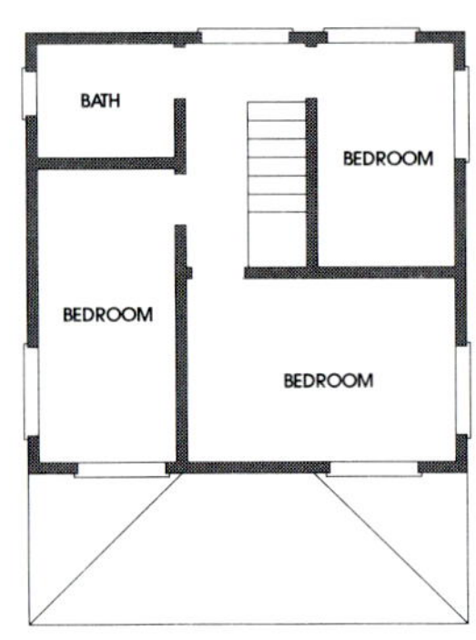

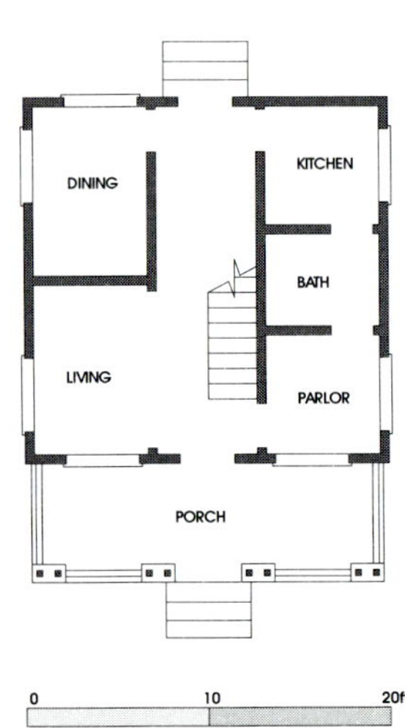

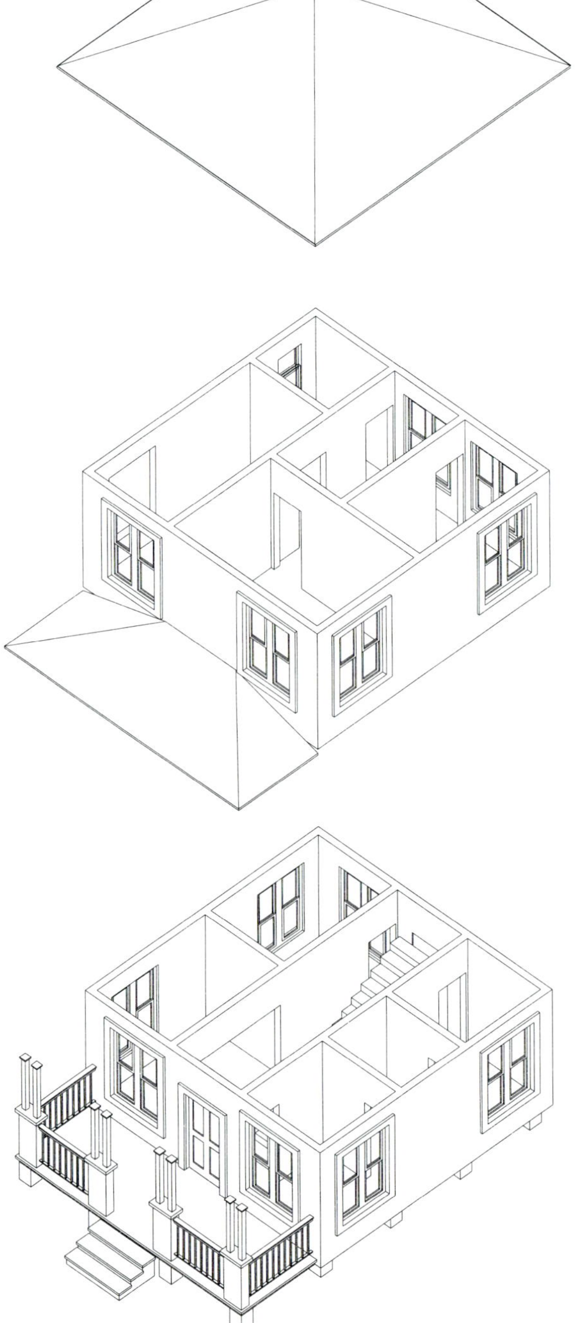

FLOOR PLANS

THE URBAN AND LANDSCAPE REGULATIONS WERE DERIVED FROM AN ANALYSIS OF SANDBORN MAPS, HISTORIC AMERICAN BUILDING SURVEYS, AERIALS, SITE VISITS, AND CONVERSATIONS WITH LOCAL RESIDENTS, HISTORIC PRESERVATION GROUPS, ARCHITECTS, LANDSCAPE ARCHITECTS, TRAFFIC ENGINEERS, SCHOOLS OF ARCHITECTURE AND PLANNING, AND ZONING DEPARTMENTS.

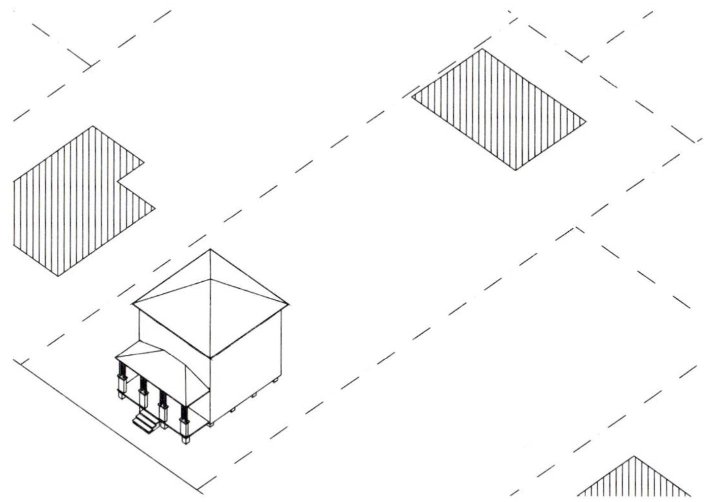

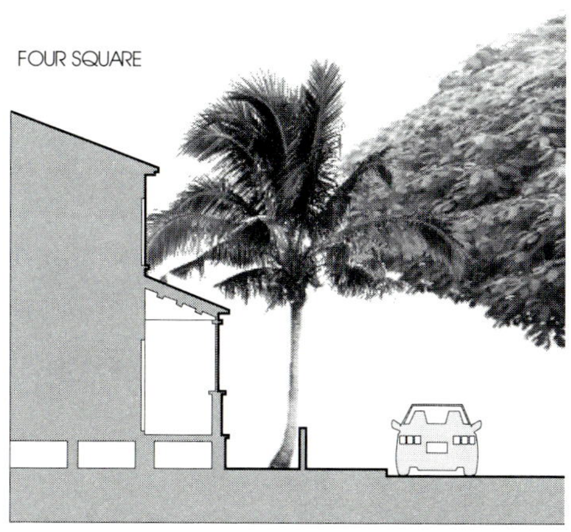

URBAN REGULATIONS

PLACEMENT

: 20 % MAXIMUM BUILDING LOT COVERAGE
: 65 % MINIMUM PERVIOUS AREA
: 65 % MINIMUM STREET FRONTAGE BUILD-OUT
: 15 FT MINIMUM FRONT YARD
: 5 FT MINIMUM SIDE STREET YARD
: 30 FT MINIMUM REAR YARD

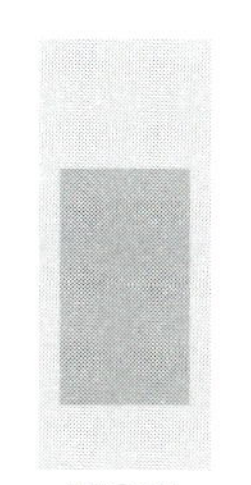

ENCROACHMENT

: 6 FT MINIMUM DEPTH FRONT PORCH REQUIRED AND 100% MINIMUM WIDTH

PARKING / OUTBUILDING

: TWO CAR SPACE ALLOWED
: 20 FT X 20 FT MAXIMUM LOT COVERAGE
: 4 FT MINIMUM SIDE YARD SETBACKS, PARKING
: 5 FT MINIMUM SIDE AND REAR YARD SETBACKS, OUTBUILDING

HEIGHT & USE

: 22 FT MAXIMUM MAIN BUILDING EAVE
: 12 FT MAXIMUM PORCH EAVE
: FIRST FLOOR RESIDENTIAL
: SECOND FLOOR RESIDENTIAL

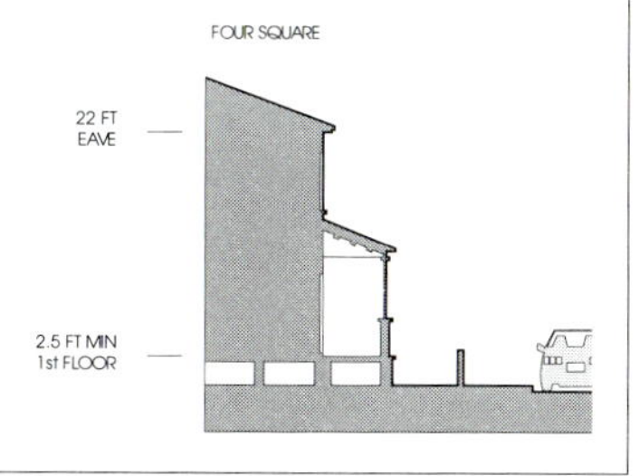

LANDSCAPE REGULATIONS

FRONT YARD

: *MAY BE PLANTED WITH SHRUBS, HEDGES, FLOWERS AND/OR GRASS*
: *LAWN AREA 30% MINIMUM OF THE TOTAL LOT AREA*
: *VINES MAY BE PLANTED TO GROW ON PORCHES*

PERIMETER

: A CONTINUOUS HEDGE IS REQUIRED AT A MINIMUM OF 6 FT HEIGHT AT THE SIDES & REAR
: DEPENDING ON THE STREET TYPE, THE FRONT ELEVATION MAY BE SCREENED WITH TREES AND PALMS

DRIVEWAY

: MAY BE PLANTED WITH SHRUBS, HEDGES, FLOWERS AND/OR GRASS
: 20 FT MAXIMUM WIDTH
: SHALL BE A STRAIGHT, PERPENDICULAR PAVED AREA RUNNING FROM THE STREET TO PARKING

RIGHT-OF-WAY

: MAY BE PLANTED WITH PALMS AND TREES
: UNPAVED AREAS SHALL BE PLANTED WITH GRASS

Conch Mansion:

This building type is a single family two story home with a deep front porch embracing two sides of the home; a one room wide footprint plus a side hallway; a comfortable private rear yard, and, on-site parking. The L-shape plan is organized around the side hall. The building is substantially raised on a retention wall and a pier foundation to allow for air circulation, flooding recharge and privacy.

The common building name is a "Victorian House."

Case Studies:

ADDRESS	: 701 Fleming Street
	: 703 Fleming Street

STREET VIEW

BLOCK

BLOCK TYPE:

BLOCK	: 350 ft X 400 ft
TOTAL LOTS	: 20
CORNER	: 8 ft radius

STREET TYPE:

SPATIAL RATIO	: 1:3 (Height to Width)
R.O.W.	: 50 ft
LANE(S)	: Two lanes, one way
PARKING	: Parallel, two sides
SIDEWALK	: 10 ft, both sides
LANDSCAPE	: Tropical
STREETSCAPE	: Lamp post
SIGNAGE	: Posted on main structure
ELECTRICITY	: Overhead wiring
USE	: Mixed-Use
ORIENTATION	: Southeast

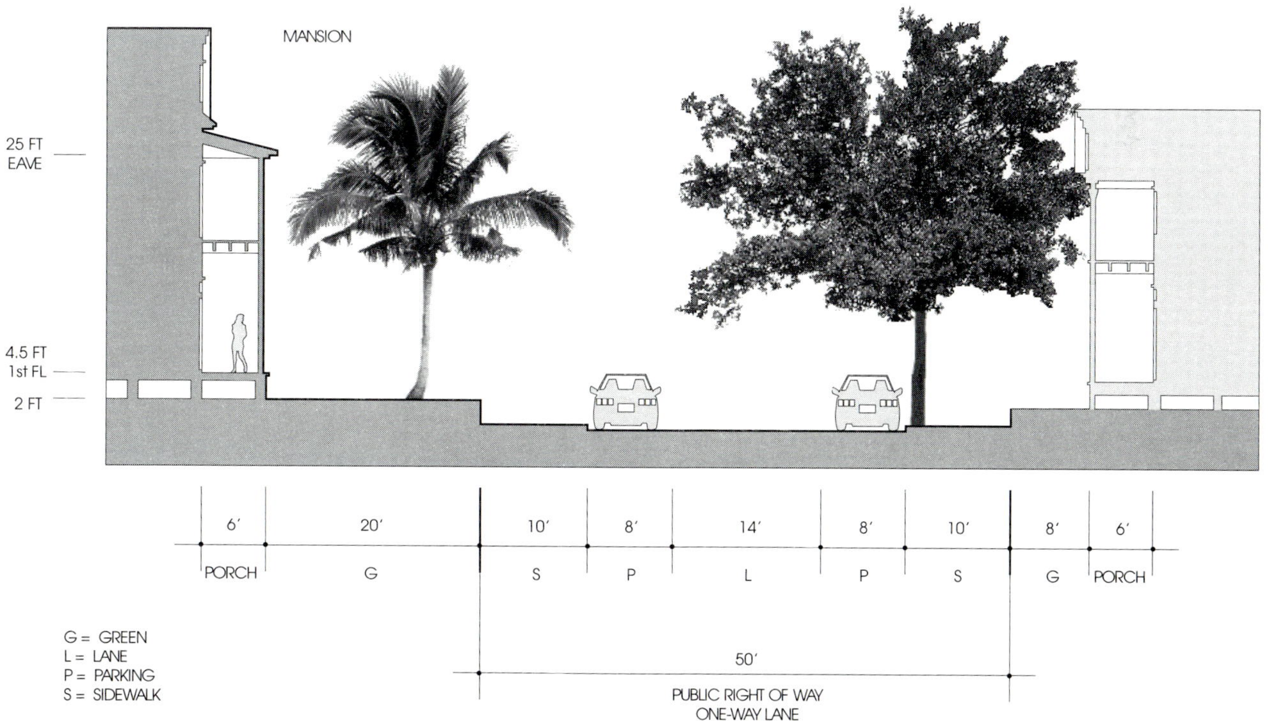

STREET SECTION THROUGH SOUTHARD STREET

Lot Type:

TYPE	: Corner yard
COVERAGE	: 20 %
F.A.R.	: 40 %
PERVIOUS AREA	: 65 %
SIZE	: 50 ft X 115 ft
PARKING	: Two car space
FRONT YARD	: 26 ft
SIDE YARD	: 10 ft
REAR YARD	: 40 ft
ENCROACHMENT	: 6 ft maximum, with open structure
OUTBUILDING	: In the rear yard
FENCE	: 4 ft high front and 6 ft high sides and rear
DRIVEWAY	: Width 18 maximum, perpendicular to street

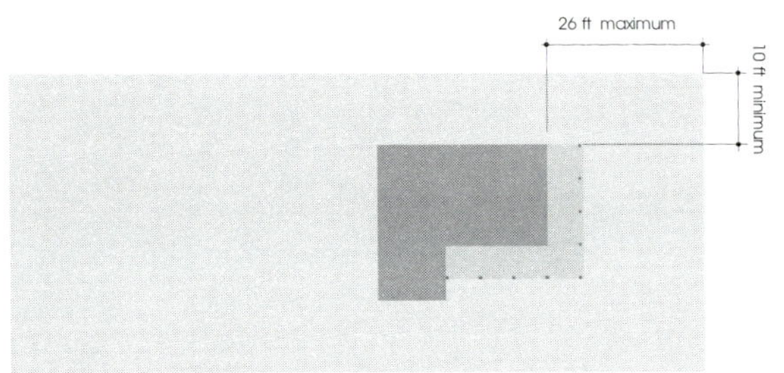

BUILDING LOT

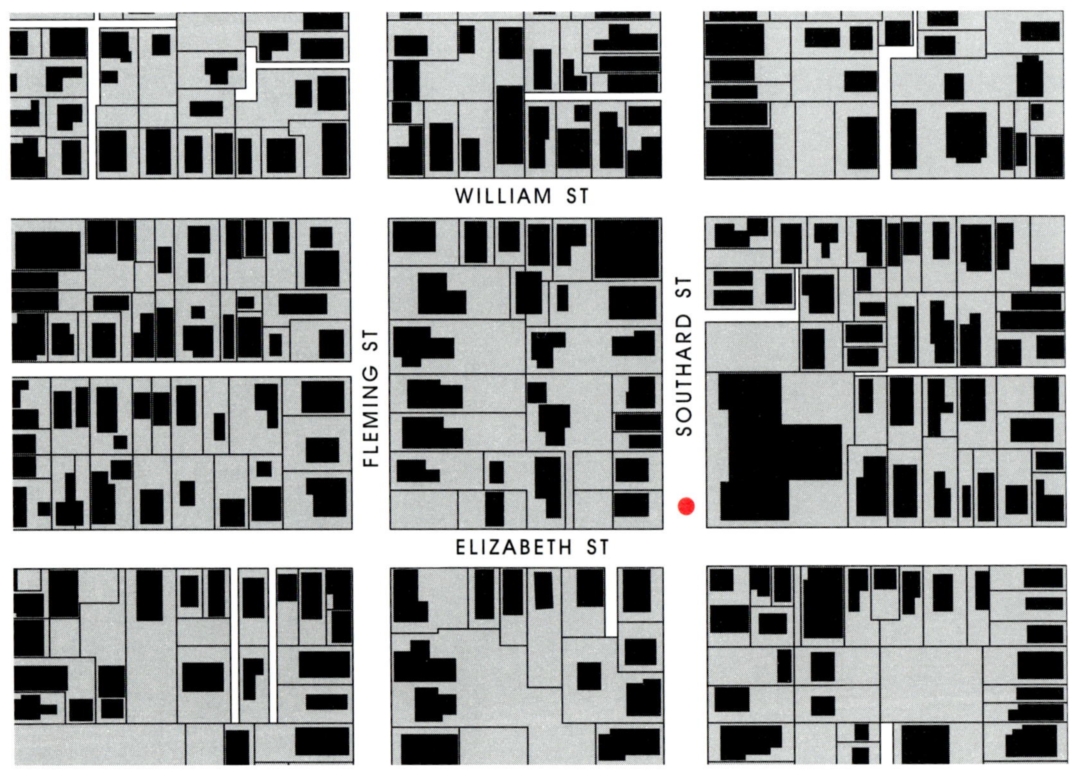

LOCATION MAP

FRONT ELEVATION

BUILDING TYPE:

CONSTRUCTION	: Wood frame
USE	: Residential
UNITS/ACRE	: 43
FACADE ASPECT	: Porch
PORCH	: 6 ft
CLIMATE CONTROL	: Deep porch for screening the sun, air vents and double hung windows for natural ventilation
SECURITY	: Public rooms and main entrance off the sidewalk
WINDOW/DOOR	: Vertical proportions

BUILDING FINISH:

WALLS	: Wood siding
ROOF	: Metal shingles or V-crimp
COLOR	: White, light gray or pastel shades
PRIVACY	: Fences and raised floor

TYPICAL PEDESTRIAN VIEW

PLAN TYPE:

CHARACTERISTIC	: Central hall
SHAPE	: Square
FOOTPRINT	: 26 ft X 28 ft
SQUARE FOOTAGE	: 2185 sq ft
1ST LEVEL	: 4.5 ft above the sidewalk
ORIENTATION	: Perpendicular to main street
KITCHEN	: 1st floor, overlooking rear yard
DINING ROOM	: 1st floor, overlooking sidewalk
LIVING ROOM	: 1st floor, overlooking sidewalk
BEDROOM(S)	: 2nd & 3rd floors
YARD	: Semi-public front, private rear
OUTBUILDING	: None

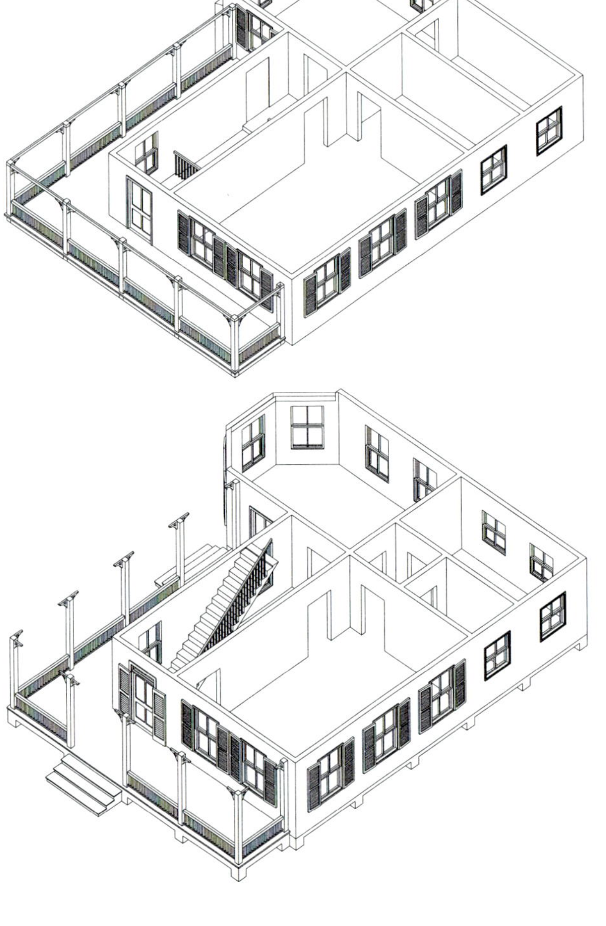

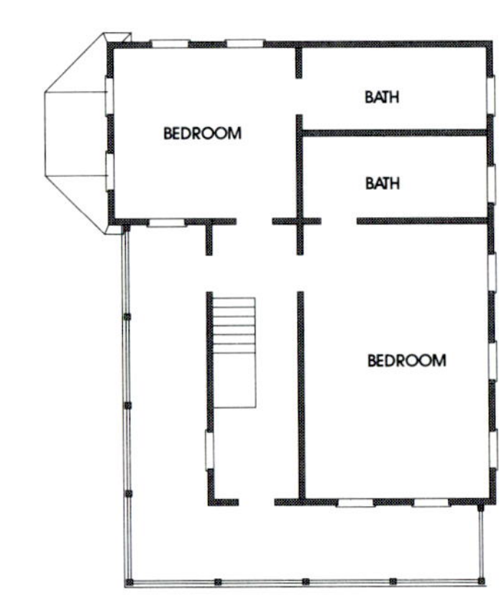

SECOND FLOOR PLAN

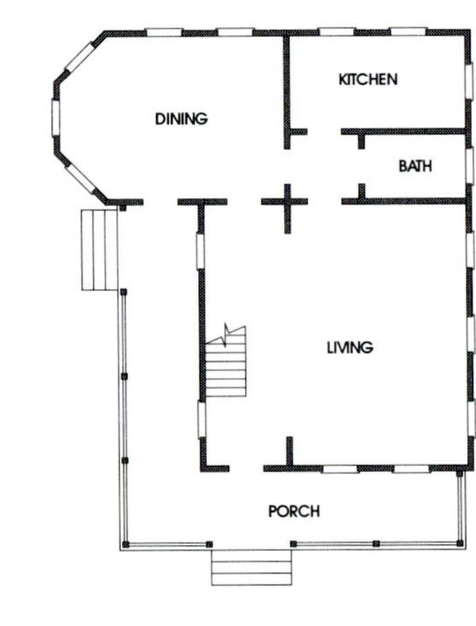

FIRST FLOOR PLAN

0 10 30ft

FLOOR PLANS

THE URBAN AND LANDSCAPE REGULATIONS WERE DERIVED FROM AN ANALYSIS OF SANDBORN MAPS, HISTORIC AMERICAN BUILDING SURVEYS, AERIALS, SITE VISITS, AND CONVERSATIONS WITH LOCAL RESIDENTS, HISTORIC PRESERVATION GROUPS, ARCHITECTS, LANDSCAPE ARCHITECTS, TRAFFIC ENGINEERS, SCHOOLS OF ARCHITECTURE AND PLANNING, AND ZONING DEPARTMENTS.

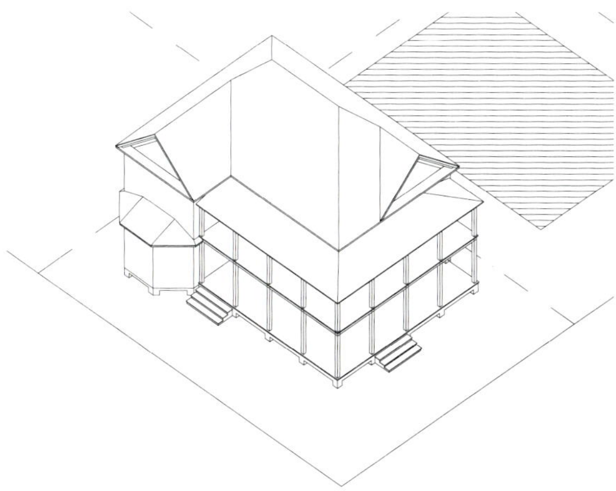

URBAN REGULATIONS

PLACEMENT

: 20 % MAXIMUM BUILDING LOT COVERAGE
: 65 % MINIMUM PERVIOUS AREA
: 50 % MINIMUM STREET FRONTAGE BUILD-OUT
: 26 FT MINIMUM FRONT YARD
: 10 FT MINIMUM SIDE YARD
: 40 FT MINIMUM REAR YARD

ENCROACHMENT

: 6 FT MINIMUM DEPTH FRONT PORCH REQUIRED AND 90% MINIMUM WIDTH

PARKING / OUTBUILDING

: TWO CAR SPACE ALLOWED
: 2 FT MINIMUM REAR YARD
: 10 FT MINIMUM SIDE YARD

HEIGHT & USE

: 28 FT MAXIMUM MAIN BUILDING EAVE
: 25 FT MAXIMUM PORCH EAVE
: FIRST FLOOR RESIDENTIAL
: SECOND FLOOR AND ABOVE RESIDENTIAL

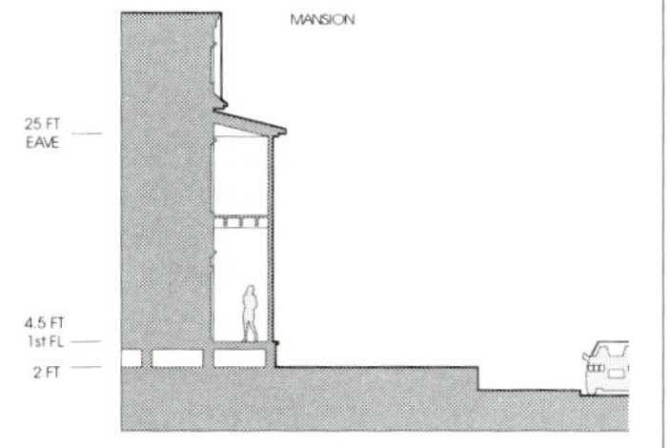

LANDSCAPE REGULATIONS

FRONT YARD

: *MAY BE PLANTED WITH SHRUBS, HEDGES, FLOWERS AND/OR GRASS*
: *LAWN AREA 30% MINIMUM OF THE TOTAL LOT AREA*
: *VINES MAY BE PLANTED TO GROW ON PORCHES*

PERIMETER

: A CONTINUOUS HEDGE IS REQUIRED AT A MINIMUM OF 6 FT HEIGHT AT THE SIDES & REAR
: DEPENDING ON THE STREET TYPE, THE FRONT ELEVATION MAY BE SCREENED WITH TREES AND PALMS

DRIVEWAY

: MAY BE PLANTED WITH SHRUBS, HEDGES, FLOWERS AND/OR GRASS
: 20 FT MAXIMUM WIDTH
: SHALL BE A STRAIGHT, PERPENDICULAR PAVED AREA RUNNING FROM THE STREET TO PARKING

RIGHT-OF-WAY

: MAY BE PLANTED WITH PALMS AND TREES
: UNPAVED AREAS SHALL BE PLANTED WITH GRASS

Conch Guest House:

This building type is a three story home with a front porch that runs parallel to the street; a footprint that is four-room wide with a central hallway; a comfortable private side yard; and, on-site parking. The plan is organized around a central hall that runs the entire depth of the building. Similar to the "Eyebrow", this building shades the third floor windows with its front porch and continuous two story high columns. The building is raised on a pier foundation to allow for air circulation, flooding recharge and privacy.

The common building name is "Classic Revival Six-Bay, Two-And-A-Half-Story."

Case Study:

ADDRESS : 601 Caroline Street

STREET VIEW

ELIZABETH ST
GREENE ST
CAROLINE ST
SIMONTON ST

BLOCK

Block Type:

BLOCK	: Typical dimension 400 ft X 400 ft
TOTAL LOTS	: 24
CORNER	: 8 ft radius

Street Type:

SPATIAL RATIO	: 1:2 (Height to Width)
R.O.W.	: 50 ft
LANE(S)	: Two lanes, one way
PARKING	: Parallel, both sides
SIDEWALK	: 10 ft, both sides
LANDSCAPE	: Tropical
STREETSCAPE	: Lamp post
SIGNAGE	: Posted on main structure
ELECTRICITY	: Overhead wiring
USE	: Mixed-Use
ORIENTATION	: Southeast

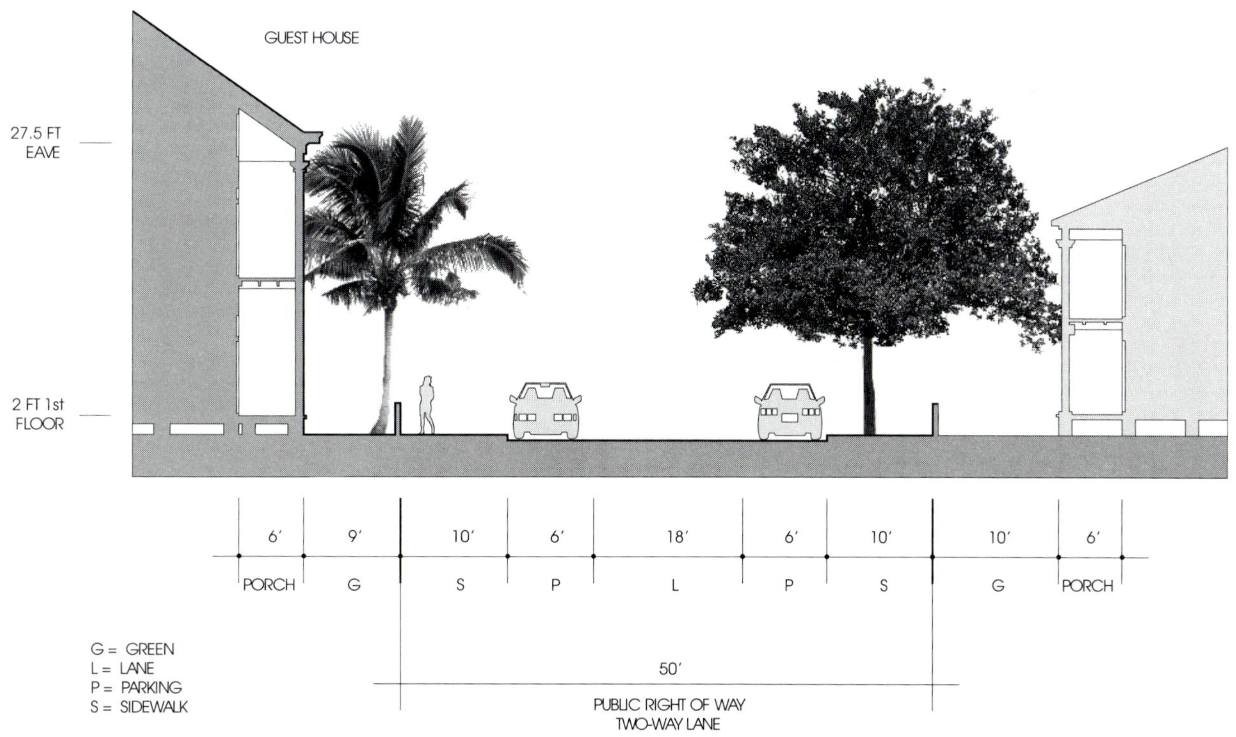

STREET SECTION THROUGH CAROLINE STREET

Lot Type:

TYPE	: Side yard
COVERAGE	: 30 %
F.A.R.	: 90 %
PERVIOUS AREA	: 65 %
SIZE	: 50 ft X 90 ft
PARKING	: Two car parking on site.
FRONT YARD	: 12 ft
SIDE YARD	: 5 ft
REAR YARD	: 10 ft
ENCROACHMENT	: 6 ft maximum, with open structure
OUTBUILDING	: In the side yard
FENCE	: 4 ft high front and 6 ft high sides and rear
DRIVEWAY	: Width 10 ft maximum, perpendicular to street

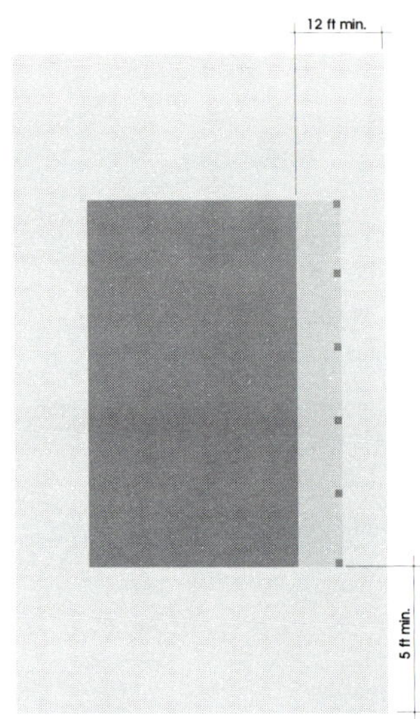

BUILDING LOT

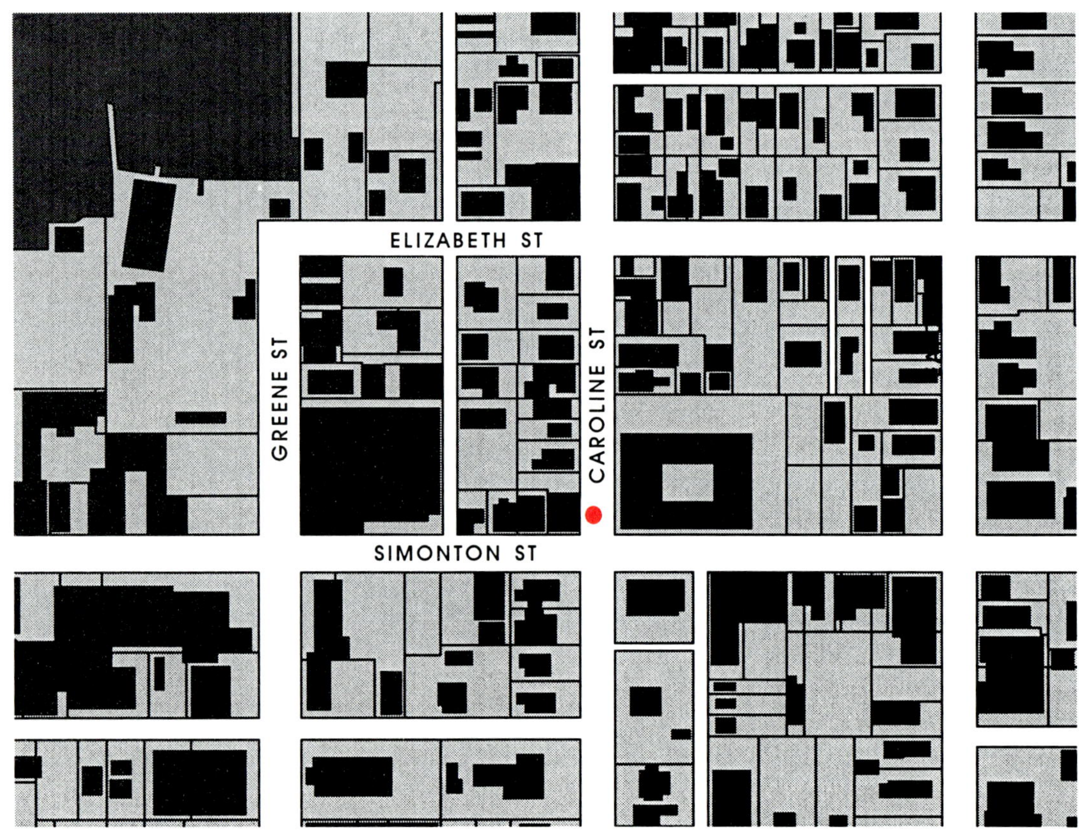

LOCATION MAP

FRONT ELEVATION

BUILDING TYPE:

CONSTRUCTION	: Wood frame
USE	: Residential
UNITS/ACRE	: 10
FACADE ASPECT	: Porch
PORCH	: 6 ft
CLIMATE CONTROL	: Deep porch for screening the sun, air vents and double hung windows for natural ventilation
SECURITY	: Public rooms and main entrance off the sidewalk
WINDOW/DOOR	: Vertical proportions

BUILDING FINISH:

WALLS	: Wood siding
ROOF	: Metal shingles or V-crimp
COLOR	: White, light gray or pastel shades
PRIVACY	: Fences, raised floor and landscaping

PEDESTRIAN VIEW

PLAN TYPE:

CHARACTERISTIC	: Central hall
SHAPE	: Rectangular
FOOTPRINT	: 50 ft X 28 ft
SQUARE FOOTAGE	: 4000 to 4500 sq ft
FIRST LEVEL	: 2 ft above the sidewalk
ORIENTATION	: Parallel to main street
KITCHEN	: 1st floor, overlooking rear yard
DINING ROOM	: 1st floor, overlooking sidewalk
LIVING ROOM	: 1st floor, overlooking sidewalk
BEDROOM(S)	: 2nd & 3rd floors
YARD	: Semi-public front, private rear
OUTBUILDING	: None

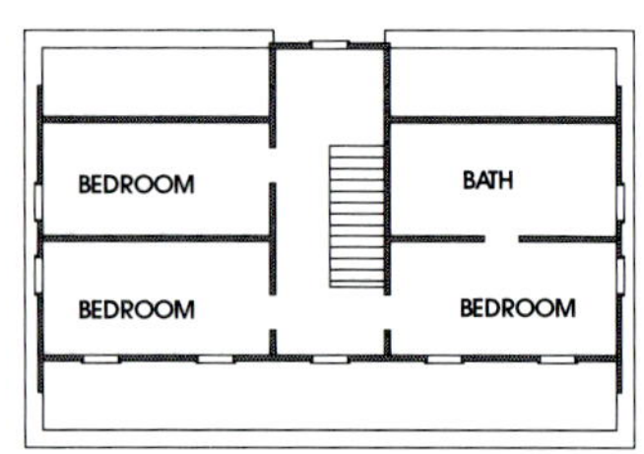

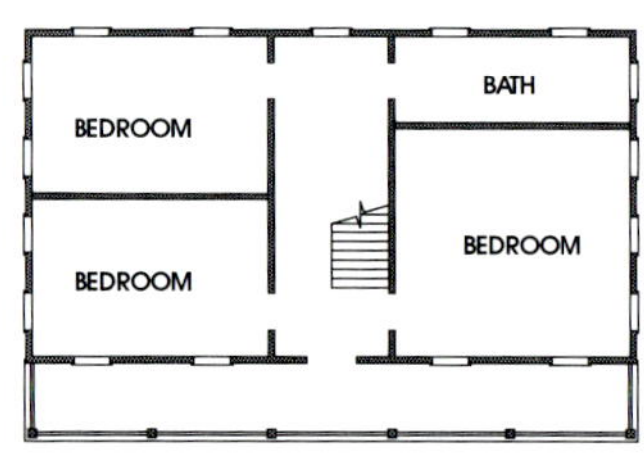

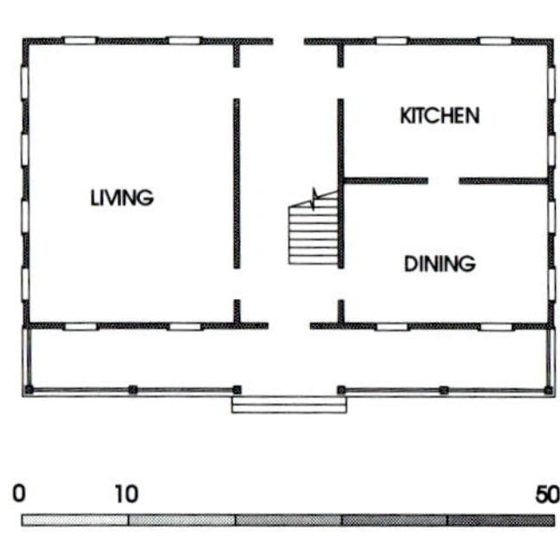

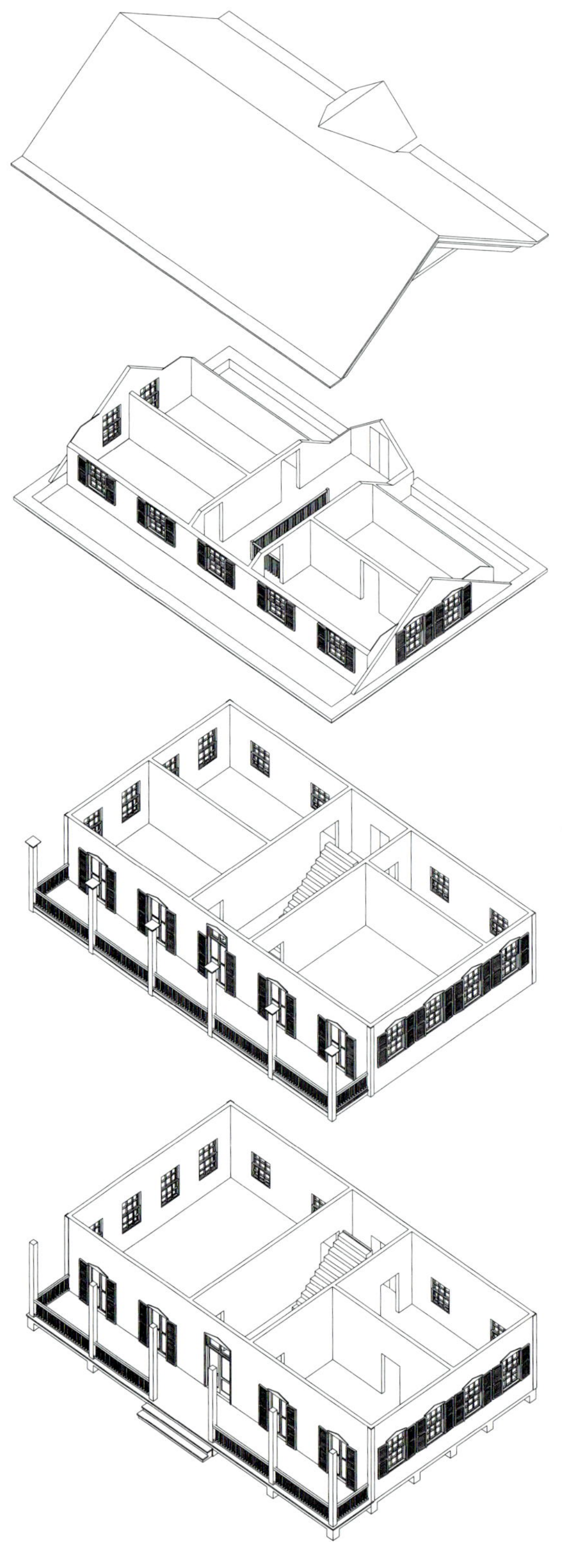

FLOOR PLANS

THE URBAN AND LANDSCAPE REGULATIONS WERE DERIVED FROM AN ANALYSIS OF SANDBORN MAPS, HISTORIC AMERICAN BUILDING SURVEYS, AERIALS, SITE VISITS, AND CONVERSATIONS WITH LOCAL RESIDENTS, HISTORIC PRESERVATION GROUPS, ARCHITECTS, LANDSCAPE ARCHITECTS, TRAFFIC ENGINEERS, SCHOOLS OF ARCHITECTURE AND PLANNING, AND ZONING DEPARTMENTS.

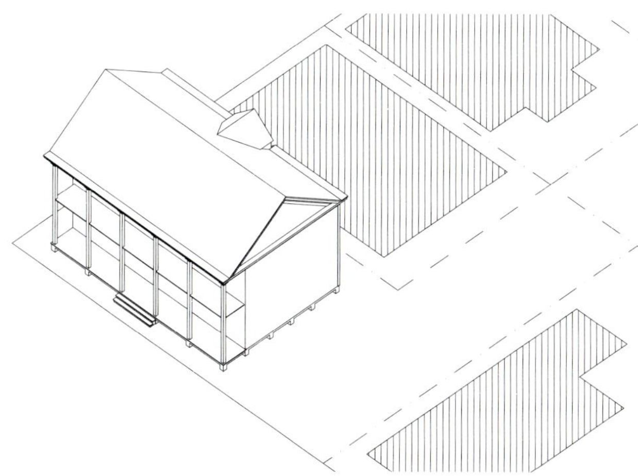

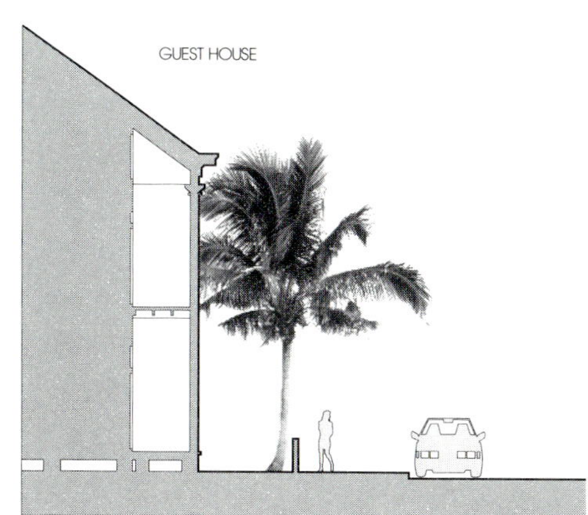

URBAN REGULATIONS

Placement

: 30 % MAXIMUM BUILDING LOT COVERAGE
: 65 % MINIMUM PERVIOUS AREA
: 60 % MINIMUM STREET FRONTAGE BUILD-OUT
: 12 FT MINIMUM FRONT YARD
: 5 FT MINIMUM SIDE YARD
: 10 FT MINIMUM REAR YARD

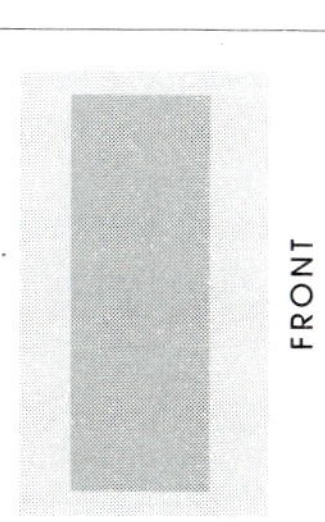

Encroachment

: 6 FT MINIMUM DEPTH FRONT PORCH REQUIRED AND 100% MINIMUM WIDTH

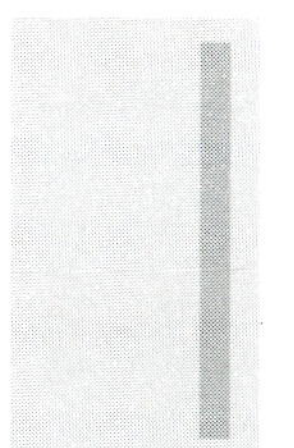

Parking / Outbuilding

: TWO CAR SPACE ALLOWED
: 20 FT X 20 FT MAXIMUM
: 5 FT MINIMUM SIDE YARD

Height & Use

: 27.5 FT MAXIMUM BUILDING EAVE
: FIRST FLOOR RESIDENTIAL
: SECOND FLOOR AND ABOVE RESIDENTIAL

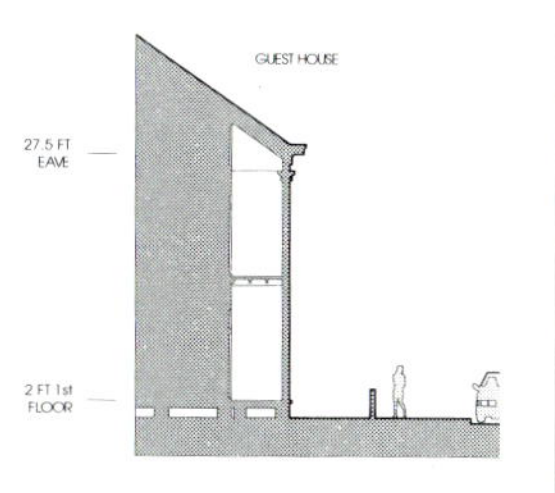

LANDSCAPE REGULATIONS

Front Yard

: *MAY BE PLANTED WITH SHRUBS, HEDGES, FLOWERS AND/OR GRASS*
: *LAWN AREA 30% MINIMUM OF THE TOTAL LOT AREA*
: *VINES MAY BE PLANTED TO GROW ON PORCHES*

Perimeter

: A CONTINUOUS HEDGE IS REQUIRED AT A MINIMUM OF 6 FT HEIGHT AT THE SIDES & REAR
: DEPENDING ON THE STREET TYPE, THE FRONT ELEVATION MAY BE SCREENED WITH TREES AND PALMS

Driveway

: MAY BE PLANTED WITH SHRUBS, HEDGES, FLOWERS AND/OR GRASS
: 20 FT MAXIMUM WIDTH
: SHALL BE A STRAIGHT, PERPENDICULAR PAVED AREA RUNNING FROM THE STREET TO PARKING

Right-Of-Way

: MAY BE PLANTED WITH PALMS AND TREES
: UNPAVED AREAS SHALL BE PLANTED WITH GRASS

Conch Six-bay:

This building type is a two story house with a front porch embracing two sides; a two room wide footprint plus a central hallway; a comfortable private side yard; and, on-site parking. The plan is organized around a central hall running the entire depth of the main structure. This building has a second structure attached to rear side. The building is raised on a pier foundation to allow for air circulation, flooding recharge and privacy.

The common building name is "Classic Revival Six Bay, Two-Story."

Case Study:

ADDRESS : 603 Southard Street

STREET VIEW

BLOCK

Block Type:

BLOCK	: Typical dimension 400 ft X 460 ft
TOTAL LOTS	: 40
CORNER	: 8 ft radius

Street Type:

SPATIAL RATIO	: 1:3 (Height to Width)
R.O.W.	: 50 ft
LANE(S)	: Two lanes, one way
PARKING	: Parallel, two sides
SIDEWALK	: 10 ft, both sides
LANDSCAPE	: Tropical
STREETSCAPE	: Lamp post
SIGNAGE	: Posted on main structure
ELECTRICITY	: Overhead wiring
USE	: Mixed-Use
ORIENTATION	: Southeast

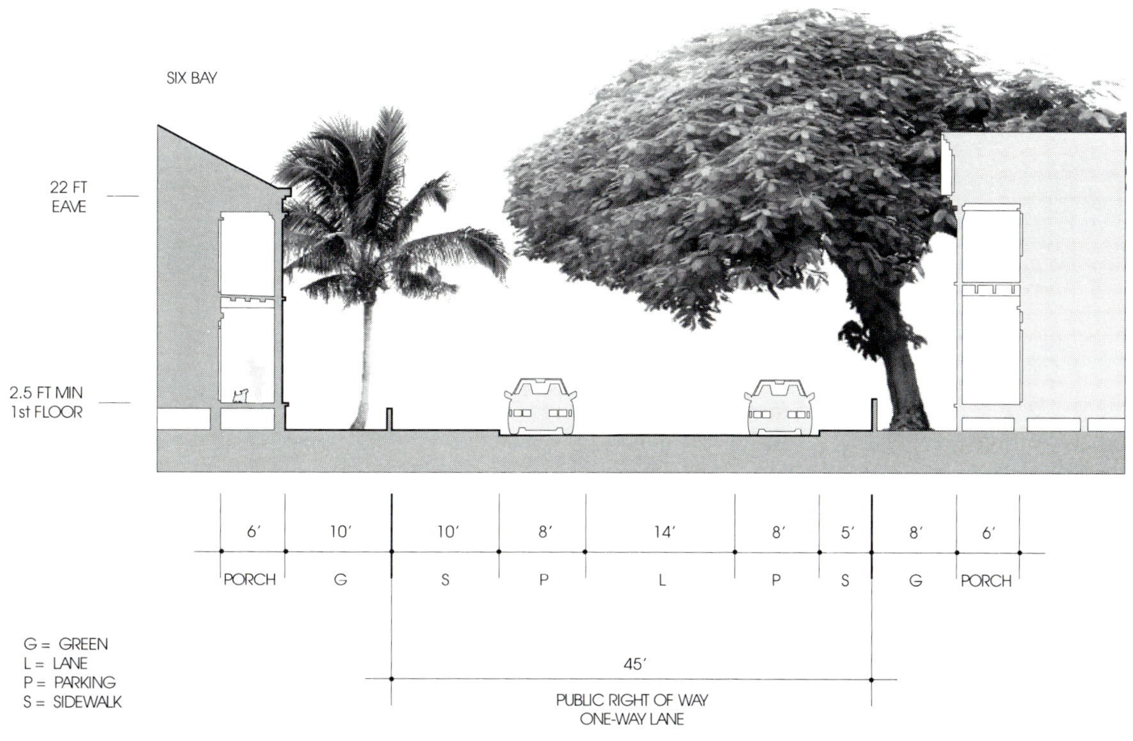

STREET SECTION THROUGH SOUTHARD STREET

Lot Type:

TYPE	: Front yard
COVERAGE	: 40 %
F.A.R.	: 40 %
PERVIOUS AREA	: 65 %
SIZE	: 100 ft X 65 ft
PARKING	: Two car parking on site.
FRONT YARD	: 15 ft
SIDE YARD	: 10 ft
REAR YARD	: 10 ft
ENCROACHMENT	: 6 ft maximum, with open structure
OUTBUILDING	: None
FENCE	: 4 ft high front and 6 ft high sides and rear
DRIVEWAY	: Width 10 ft maximum, perpendicular to street

15 ft min.

10 ft min.

BUILDING LOT

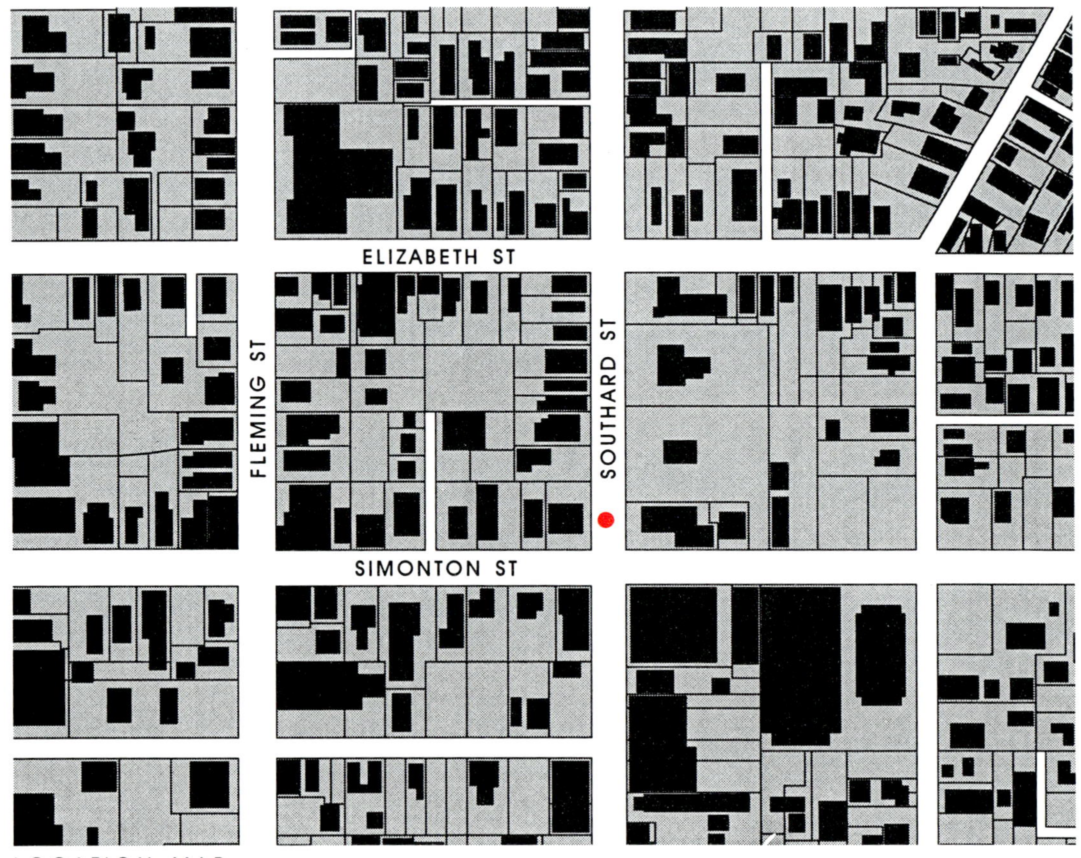

LOCATION MAP

FRONT ELEVATION

Building Type:

CONSTRUCTION	: Wood frame
USE	: Residential
UNITS/ACRE	: 6.7
FACADE ASPECT	: Porch
PORCH	: 6 ft
CLIMATE CONTROL	: Deep porch for screening the sun, air vents and double hung windows for natural ventilation
SECURITY	: Public rooms and main entrance off the sidewalk
WINDOW/DOOR	: Vertical proportions

Building Finish:

WALLS	: Wood siding
ROOF	: Metal shingles or V-crimp
COLOR	: White, light gray or pastel shades
PRIVACY	: Fences, raised floor and landscaping

PEDESTRIAN VIEW

Plan Type:

CHARACTERISTIC	: Central hall
SHAPE	: Rectangular
FOOTPRINT	: 40 ft X 45 ft
SQUARE FOOTAGE	: 2500 to 3000 sq ft
1ST LEVEL	: 4.5 ft above the sidewalk
ORIENTATION	: Parallel to main street
KITCHEN	: 1st floor, overlooking garden
DINING ROOM	: 1st floor, overlooking sidewalk
LIVING ROOM	: 1st floor, overlooking sidewalk
SLEEPING ROOM	: 2nd floor
YARD	: Semi-public front, private rear
OUTBUILDING	: Attached to the main structure

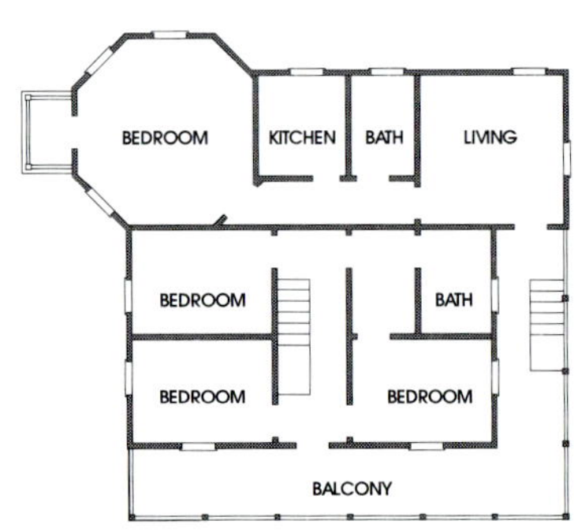

SECOND FLOOR

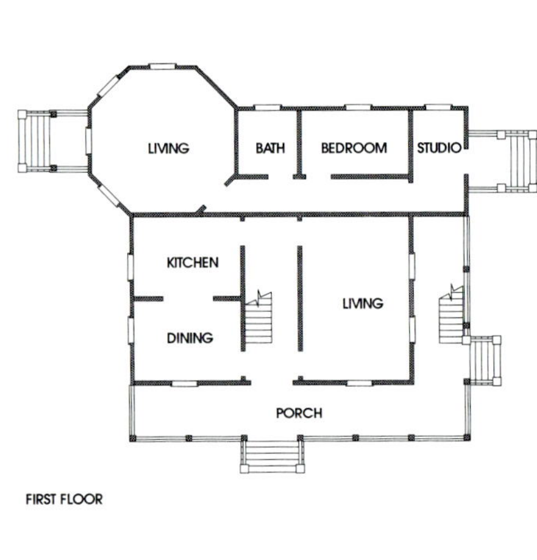

FIRST FLOOR

0 10 40ft

FLOOR PLANS

THE URBAN AND LANDSCAPE REGULATIONS WERE DERIVED FROM AN ANALYSIS OF SANBORN MAPS, HISTORIC AMERICAN BUILDING SURVEYS, AERIALS, SITE VISITS, AND CONVERSATIONS WITH LOCAL RESIDENTS, HISTORIC PRESERVATION GROUPS, ARCHITECTS, LANDSCAPE ARCHITECTS, TRAFFIC ENGINEERS, SCHOOLS OF ARCHITECTURE AND PLANNING AND ZONING DEPARTMENTS.

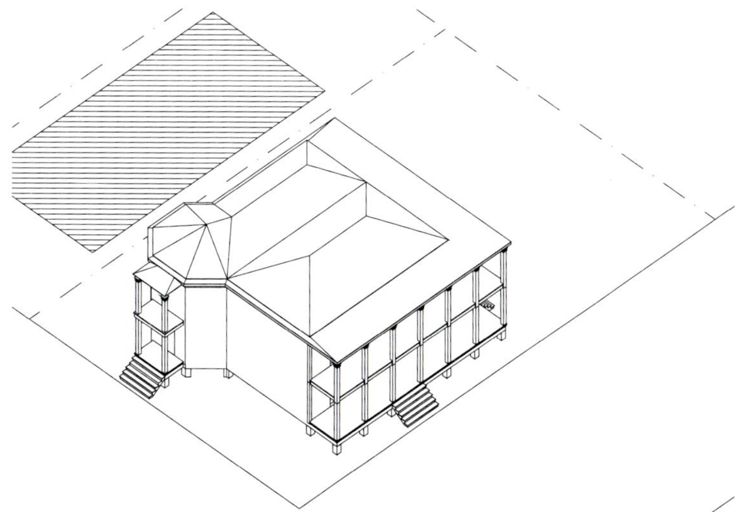

URBAN REGULATIONS

PLACEMENT

: 40 % MAXIMUM BUILDING LOT COVERAGE
: 35 % MINIMUM STREET FRONTAGE BUILD-OUT
: 65 % MINIMUM PERVIOUS AREA
: 15 FT MINIMUM FRONT YARD
: 10 FT MINIMUM SIDE YARD
: 10 FT MINIMUM REAR YARD

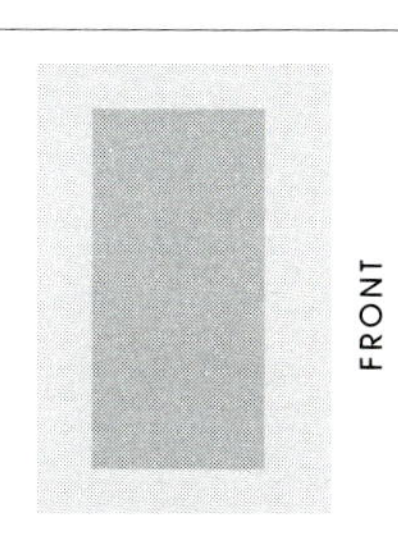

ENCROACHMENT

: 6 FT MINIMUM DEPTH FRONT PORCH REQUIRED AND 100 % MINIMUM WIDTH

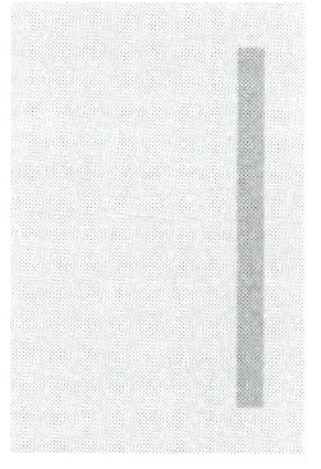

PARKING / OUTBUILDING

: TWO CAR SPACE ALLOWED
: 20 FT X 20 FT MAXIMUM, PARKING
: 10 FT MINIMUM SIDE YARD

HEIGHT & USE

: 24 FT MAXIMUM MAIN BUILDING EAVE
: 22 FT MAXIMUM PORCH EAVE
: FIRST FLOOR RESIDENTIAL
: SECOND FLOOR AND ABOVE RESIDENTIAL

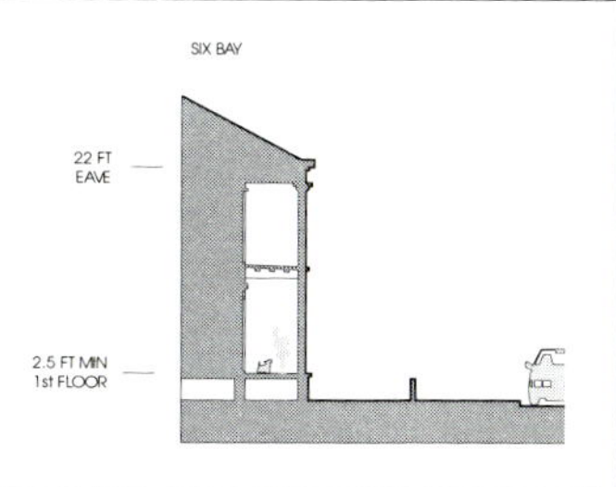

LANDSCAPE REGULATIONS

FRONT YARD

: *MAY BE PLANTED WITH SHRUBS, HEDGES, FLOWERS AND/OR GRASS*
: *LAWN AREA 30% MINIMUM OF THE TOTAL LOT AREA*
: *VINES MAY BE PLANTED TO GROW ON PORCHES*

PERIMETER

: A CONTINUOUS HEDGE IS REQUIRED AT A MINIMUM OF 5 FT HEIGHT AT THE SIDES & REAR
: DEPENDING ON THE STREET TYPE, THE FRONT ELEVATION MAY BE SCREENED WITH TREES AND PALMS

DRIVEWAY

: MAY BE PLANTED WITH SHRUBS, HEDGES, FLOWERS AND/OR GRASS
: 20 FT MAXIMUM WIDTH
: SHALL BE A STRAIGHT, PERPENDICULAR PAVED AREA RUNNING FROM THE STREET TO PARKING

RIGHT-OF-WAY

: MAY BE PLANTED WITH PALMS AND TREES
: UNPAVED AREAS SHALL BE PLANTED WITH GRASS

Conch Bahama:

This building type is a two story home with a deep front porch embracing two sides; a two-room wide footprint plus a central hallway; a comfortable private rear yard; and, on-site parking. The plan is organized around a central hall. The building is raised on a pier foundation to allow for air circulation, flooding recharge and privacy. It has an addition attached to the main structure.

The common building name is "Bahama House."

Case Study:

ADDRESS : 730 Eaton Street

STREET VIEW

BLOCK

Block Type:

BLOCK	: 350 ft X 400 ft
TOTAL LOTS	: 21
CORNER	: 8 ft radius

Street Type:

SPATIAL RATIO	: 1:3 (Height to Width)
R.O.W.	: 50 ft
LANE(S)	: Two lanes, one way
PARKING	: Parallel, one side
SIDEWALK	: 10 ft, both sides
LANDSCAPE	: Tropical
STREETSCAPE	: Lamp post
SIGNAGE	: Posted on main structure
ELECTRICITY	: Overhead wiring
USE	: Mixed-Use
ORIENTATION	: Southeast

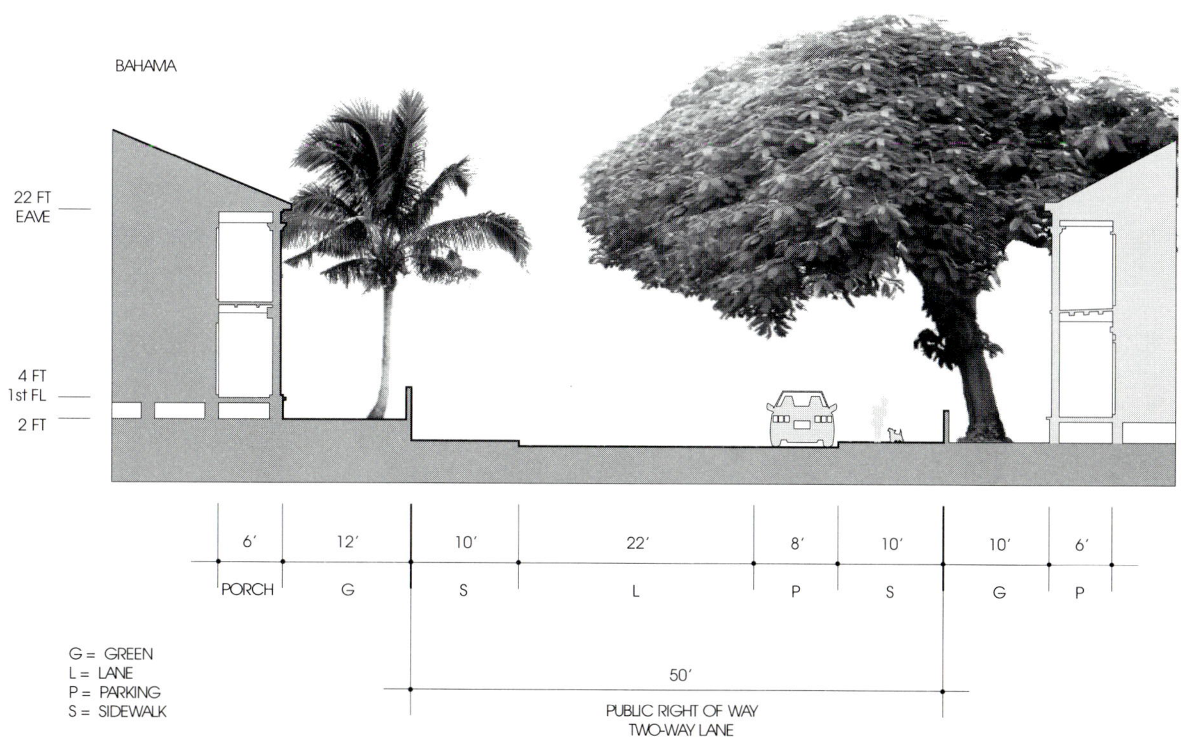

STREET SECTION THROUGH EATON STREET

Lot Type:

TYPE	: Rear yard
COVERAGE	: 40 %
F.A.R.	: 40 %
PERVIOUS AREA	: 65 %
SIZE	: 60 ft X 85 ft
PARKING	: Two car parking on site
FRONT YARD	: 16 ft
SIDE YARD	: 10 ft
REAR YARD	: 25 ft
ENCROACHMENT	: 6.5 ft maximum, with open structure
OUTBUILDING	: None
FENCE	: 4 ft high front and 6 ft high sides and rear
DRIVEWAY	: Width 12 ft maximum, perpendicular to street

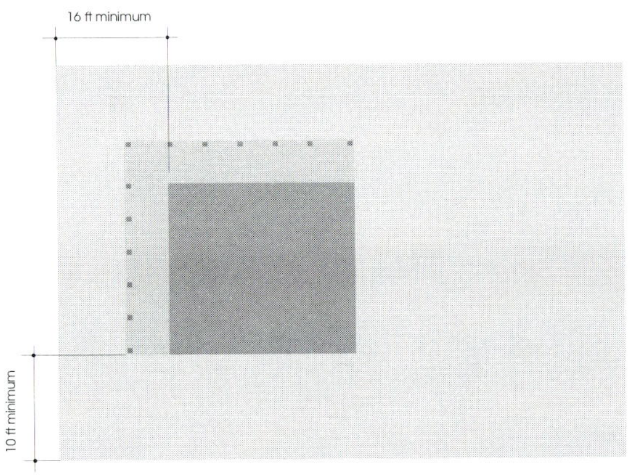

BUILDING LOT

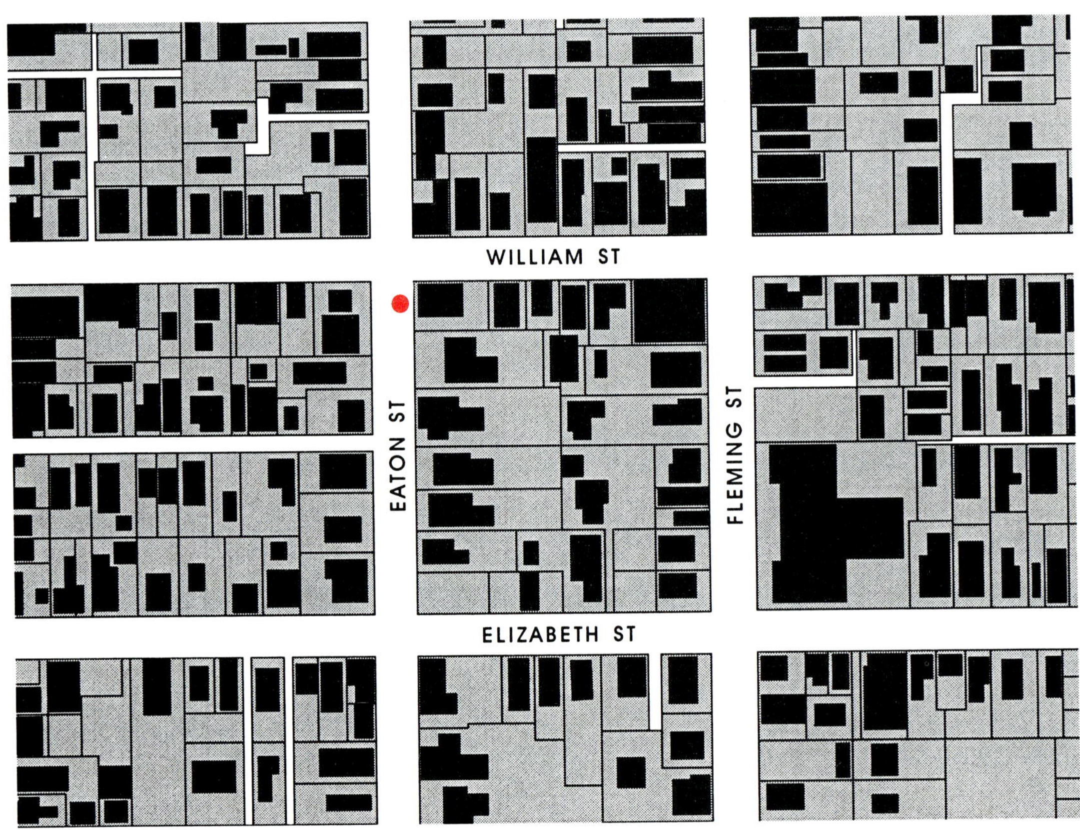

LOCATION MAP

FRONT ELEVATION

Building Type:

CONSTRUCTION	: Wood frame
USE	: Residential
UNITS/ACRE	: 17
FACADE ASPECT	: Porch
PORCH	: 6.5 ft
CLIMATE CONTROL	: Deep porch for screening the sun, air vents and full lenght windows for natural ventilation
SECURITY	: Public rooms and main entrance off the sidewalk
WINDOW/DOOR	: Vertical proportions

Building Finish:

WALLS	: Wood siding
ROOF	: Metal shingles or V-crimp
COLOR	: White, light gray or pastel shades
PRIVACY	: Fences, raised floor and land-scaping

PEDESTRIAN VIEW

PLAN TYPE:

CHARACTERISTIC	: Central hall
SHAPE	: Rectangular
FOOTPRINT	: 26 ft X 28 ft
SQUARE FOOTAGE	: 2200 to 3000 sq ft
FIRST LEVEL	: 4.5 ft above the sidewalk
ORIENTATION	: Parallel to street
KITCHEN	: 1st floor, overlooking rear yard
DINING ROOM	: 1st floor, overlooking side yard
LIVING ROOM	: 1st floor, overlooking sidewalk
BEDROOM(S)	: 2nd & 3rd floors
YARD	: Semi-public front, private rear
OUTBUILDING	: None

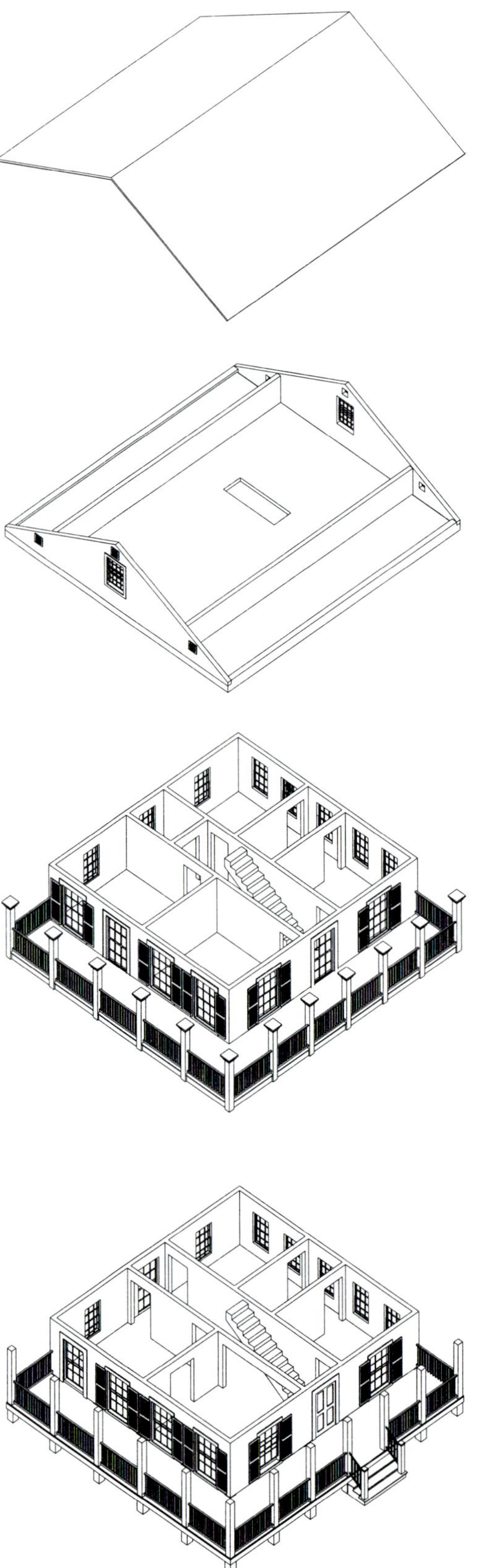

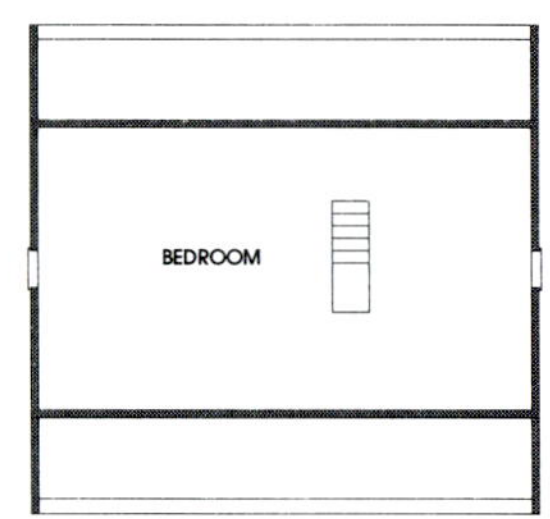

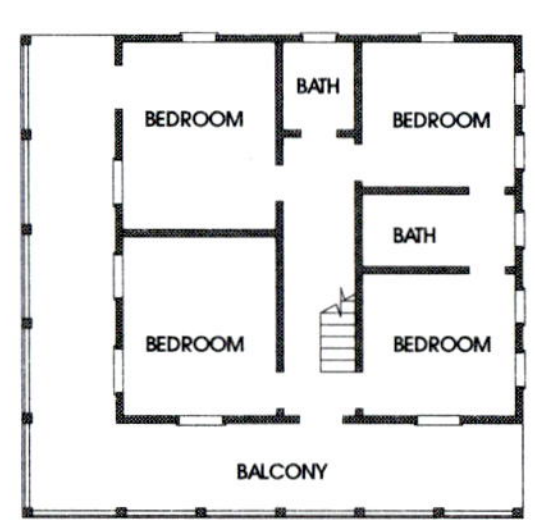

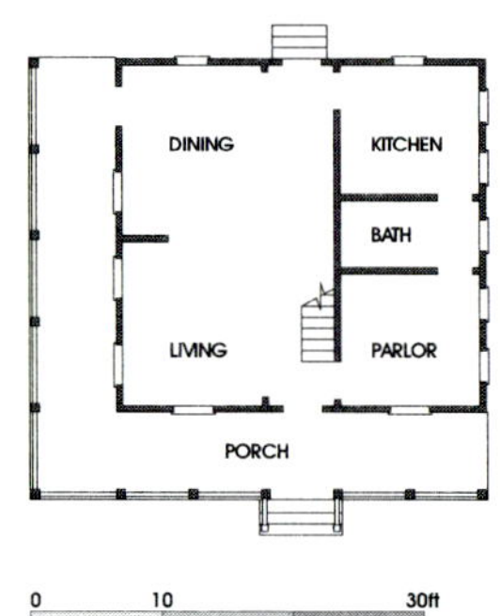

FLOOR PLANS

THE URBAN AND LANDSCAPE REGULATIONS WERE DERIVED FROM AN ANALYSIS OF SANDBORN MAPS, HISTORIC AMERICAN BUILDING SURVEYS, AERIALS, SITE VISITS, AND CONVERSATIONS WITH LOCAL RESIDENTS, HISTORIC PRESERVATION GROUPS, ARCHITECTS, LANDSCAPE ARCHITECTS, TRAFFIC ENGINEERS, SCHOOLS OF ARCHITECTURE AND PLANNING, AND ZONING DEPARTMENTS.

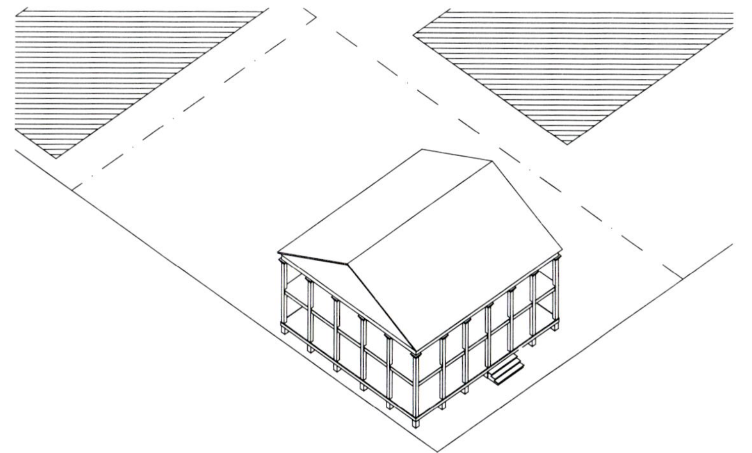

URBAN REGULATIONS

PLACEMENT

: 40 % MAXIMUM BUILDING LOT COVERAGE
: 65 % MINIMUM PERVIOUS AREA
: 40 % MINIMUM STREET FRONTAGE BUILD-OUT
: 16 FT MINIMUM FRONT YARD
: 10 FT MINIMUM SIDE YARD
: 25 FT MINIMUM REAR YARD

ENCROACHMENT

: 6.5 FT MINIMUM DEPTH FRONT PORCH REQUIRED AND 100 % MINIMUM WIDTH

PARKING / OUTBUILDING

: TWO CAR SPACE ALLOWED
: 20 FT X 20 FT MAXIMUM
: 2 FT MINIMUM REAR YARD
: 2 FT MINIMUM SIDE STREET YARD

HEIGHT & USE

: 22 FT MAXIMUM BUILDING EAVE
: FIRST FLOOR RESIDENTIAL
: SECOND FLOOR AND ABOVE RESIDENTIAL

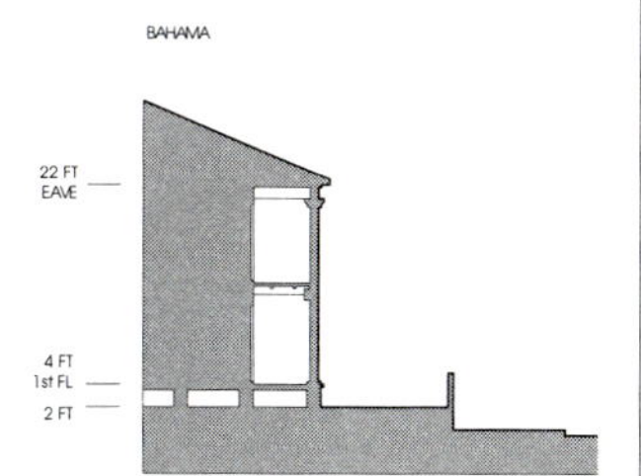

LANDSCAPE REGULATIONS

FRONT YARD

: *MAY BE PLANTED WITH SHRUBS, HEDGES, FLOWERS AND/OR GRASS*
: *LAWN AREA 30% MINIMUM OF THE TOTAL LOT AREA*
: *VINES MAY BE PLANTED TO GROW ON PORCHES*

PERIMETER

: A CONTINUOUS HEDGE IS REQUIRED AT A MINIMUM OF 6 FT HEIGHT AT THE SIDES & REAR
: DEPENDING ON THE STREET TYPE, THE FRONT ELEVATION MAY BE SCREENED WITH TREES AND PALMS

DRIVEWAY

: MAY BE PLANTED WITH SHRUBS, HEDGES, FLOWERS AND/OR GRASS
: 20 FT MAXIMUM WIDTH
: SHALL BE A STRAIGHT, PERPENDICULAR PAVED AREA RUNNING FROM THE STREET TO PARKING

RIGHT-OF-WAY

: MAY BE PLANTED WITH PALMS AND TREES
: UNPAVED AREAS SHALL BE PLANTED WITH GRASS

Landscaping also plays a vital role in establishing the character of a place. In Key West, landscaping defines two outside rooms: one public, the other private. The public room, front yard, provides a natural canopy that protects the pedestrian, bicyclist, and even cars from the harshness of the tropical climate. In the private room, rear yard, it is integrated into the Key West building.

Trees:

The trees of Key West are clearly a key to its character: From the air, the district appears camouflaged by a green blanket; From the ground, the streets maintain a natural edge and canopy.

The list below provides a comprehensive survey of the trees most commonly found, it was generated from a more detailed document available through the South Florida Water Management District.

NAME	NATURAL HEIGHT	NATIVE	DROUGHT TOLERANCE	SALT TOLERANCE	FLOWERING SEASON	FLOWER COLOR
Apple, Pitch	25'-30'	Yes	Very	Yes	Summer	Pink, White
Calabash, Black	20'-30'	Yes	Very	Yes	Spring	Yellow, Pink
Copperpod	40'-50'	No	Very	Yes	Spring, Summer	Yellow
Dogwood, Jamaican	35'-50'	Yes	Very	Yes	Spring	White, Lavender
Dragon Tree	40'-60'	No	Very	Yes	Summer	Green
Gumbo Limbo	40'-60'	Yes	Very	Moderate	Winter, Spring	Green
Magnolia, Southern	60'-100'	Yes	Very	Yes	Spring	White
Mahoe, Seaside	35'-45'	No	Very	Yes	Spring	Yellow, Red
Mahogany	35'-60'	Yes	Very	Moderate	Spring	Green, Yellow
Mangrove, Black	20'-30'	Yes		Yes	Spring	White
Oak, Live	50'-60'	Yes	Very	Yes	Spring	Green
Paradise Tree	35'-50'	Yes	Very	Moderate	Spring	White
Plum, Pigeon	25'-30'	Yes	Very	Yes	Spring	White
Pongam	30'40'	No	Very	Yes	Spring	Pink
Royal Poinciana	25'-40'	No	Very	Moderate	Summer	Red, Yellow
Tabebuia	15'	No	Very	Moderate	Spring	Yellow
Tamarind, Wild	40'-50'	Yes	Very	Yes	Spring, Summer	White

PALMS:

The palms of Key West are amongst its most memorable images. The Palms are not used to shade or provide canopy but to cast long shadows, and establish vertical elements in the landscape. The fronds of the palms have a way of play with sunlight and casting shadows that further enrich the detail of the surrounding areas.

The list below provides a comprehensive survey of the palms most commonly found, it was generated from a more detailed document available through the South Florida Water Management District.

NAME	NATURAL HEIGHT	NATIVE	DROUGHT TOLERANCE	SALT TOLERANCE	FLOWERING SEASON	FLOWER COLOR
Alexandra	40'-45'	No	Very	No	Summer	White
Areca	20'-30'	No	Very	No	Spring	White
Cabbage	45'-70'	Yes	Very	Yes	Spring, Summer	White
Canary Island Date	35'-50'	No	Very	Moderate	Spring	White
Coconut	60'-100'	No	Very	Yes	Year round	White
Florida Royal	60'-125'	Yes	Moderate	No	Spring	Yellow
Florida Thatch	15'-30'	Yes	Very	Yes	Spring, Fall	Yellow
Manilla	10'-25'	No	Very	Moderate	Summer	White
Pindo	10'-20'	No	Very	Moderate	Spring	White
Prichardia	10'-25'	No	Very	Yes	Summer	White
Paurotis	15'-25'	Yes	Moderate	Moderate	Spring	White
Silver	10'-20'	Yes	Very	Yes	Summer	White
Thatch	15'-25'	Yes	Very	Yes	Spring	White
Washington	50'-80'	No	Very	Moderate	Spring	White
Wild Date	40'-60'	No	Very	Moderate	Spring	White
Windmill	20'-40'	No	Very	Moderate	Spring	White
Key Thatch	15'-30'	Yes	Very	Yes	Spring	White

Shrubs and Hedges:

The shrubs and hedges of Key West are used to bring color into the landscape, provide security and to create privacy buffers. Considering the mixture of lot sizes, this landscape element is curiously used to express the nature of its property owner.

The list below provides a comprehensive survey of the shrubs and hedges most commonly found, it was generated from a more detailed document available through the South Florida Water Management District.

NAME	NATURAL HEIGHT	NATIVE	DROUGHT TOLERANCE	SALT TOLERANCE	FLOWERING SEASON	FLOWER COLOR
Beauty-Berry	4'-8'	Yes	Very	No	Spring	Lavender
Bougainvillea	6'-12'	No	Very	Yes	Spring, Summer	R, W, O, PU, P
Cassia, Bahama	10'-15'	Yes	Moderate	No	Summer	Yellow
Cedar, Bay	15'-20'	Yes	Very	Yes	Year round	Yellow
Cocoplum	6'-8'	Yes	Moderate	Yes	Year round	White
Coffee Colubrina	15'-20'	Yes	Very	Yes	Year round	White
Coffee, Wild	4'-6'	Yes	Moderate	No	Spring, Summer	White
Crape Myrtle	12'-15'	No	Moderate	No	Summer	W, P, R, PU
Gardenia	1'-6'	No	Moderate	No	Spring	White
Golden-Dewdrop	12'-15'	Yes	Moderate	Moderate	Spring, Summer	Blue, White
Hibiscus	6'-8'	No	Moderate	Moderate	Year round	R, Y, O, W
Jasmine, Wax	2'-3'	No	Moderate	Moderate	Year round	White
Necklace Pod	6'-10'	Yes	Moderate	Yes	Year round	Yellow
Oleander	12'-15'	No	Very	Yes	Spring, Summer	W, P, R, Y
Palm, Needle	3'-5'	Yes	Moderate	No	Spring	White
Peregrima	5'-7'	No	Very	Moderate	Year round	Red
Powderpuff	4'-6'	No	Moderate	No	Summer	R, P, W

VINES:

They help keep home's maintenance cost down. With no facade surfaces exposed, graffiti and other kinds of urban vandalism are avoided. This landscape element are used to bring color and detail into the gardens of Key West (these gardens have become an important aspect of the culture of this tropical paradise).

The list below provides a comprehensive survey of the vines most commonly found, it was generated from a more detailed document available through the South Florida Water Management District.

NAME	GROWTH RATE	NATIVE	DROUGHT TOLERANCE	SALT TOLERANCE	FLOWERING SEASON	FLOWER COLOR
Allamanda, Purple	Medium	No	Moderate	No	Summer	Purple
Bengal Clock Vine	Fast	No	Moderate	No	Spring, Summer	Blue, White
Bougainvillea	Medium	No	Very	Yes	Year round	R, P, W, O
Ceriman	Medium	No	Moderate	No	Summer	White
Coral Vine	Fast	No	Very	No	Spring, Summer	Pink
Creeping Fig	Fast	No	Very	Yes	Summer	Green
Flame Vine	Fast	No	Very	No	Winter, Spring	Orange
Garlic Vine	Medium	No	Moderate	No	Spring, Summer	L, P, W
Madagascar Rubber-vine	Medium	No	Very	Moderate	Summer, Fall	Lavender
Mandevillea, Yellow	Medium	No	Moderate	No	Summer	Yellow
Marine Ivy	Fast	Yes	Very	Yes	Summer	Green
Nepal Trumpet Flower	Medium	No	Moderate	No	Year round	Yellow
Philodendron	Fast	No	Moderate	No	Year round	Green
Rubber Vine	Medium	Yes	Moderate	Yes	Year round	White, Yelllow
Sicklethorn Vine	Medium	No	Very	No	Winter	White
Trumpet Vine	Fast	Yes	Very	No	Summer	Orange
Virginia Creeper	Fast	Yes	Very	No	Summer	White

Ground Covers and Grasses:

St. Augustine and Bermuda are common grasses found on the island of Key West. Both are salt tolerant and can average an unmowed height of 15 inches. They differ in wear, texture, and maintenance.

- Bermuda has a very good wear tolerance and fine texture but requires high mantenance.
- St. Augustine has a low wear tolerance and course texture but requires low maintenance.

The list below provides a comprehensive survey of the ground covers and grasses most commonly found, it was generated from a more detailed document available through the South Florida Water Management District.

NAME	NATURAL HEIGHT	NATIVE	DROUGHT TOLERANCE	SALT TOLERANCE	FLOWERING SEASON	FLOWER COLOR
Allamanda, Wild	12"-24"	Yes	Very	Yes	Year round	Yellow
Apple, Gopher	3"-12"	Yes	Very	Yes	Summer	Green
Asparagus Fern	12"-18"	No	Very	Moderate	SP, S, F	White
Blue Daze	10"-12"	No	Moderate	Yes	Year round	Blue
Carissa, Dwarf	12"-18"	No	Very	Yes	Summer, Fall	White
Cast Iron Plant	20"-30"	No	Moderate	Moderate	SPring	PUrple
Daylily	12"-36"	Yes	Very	Yes	SP, S, F	Y, P, O
Garlic, Society	15"-24"	No	Moderate	Moderate	Spring	PUrple
Jasmine, Confeder-ate	6"-12"	No	Moderate	Moderate	Spring	White
Juniper, Shore	12"-24"	No	Very	Yes	Spring	Green
Lantana, Dwarf	8"	Yes	Very	Moderate	Year round	Yellow
Lily Turf, Creeping	6"-18"	No	Very	Yes	Summer	PUrple, White
Peperomia	18"-20"	Yes	Very	No	Summer	Green
Periwinkle	10"-18"	No	Very	Yes	Year round	W, PU, P
Pothos	10"-12"	No	Moderate	No	Summer	Green
Purslane, Sea	12"-18"	Yes	Very	Yes	Year round	Pink
Wedelia	6"-8"	No	Very	Yes	Year round	Yellow

ONE AND A HALF STOREY

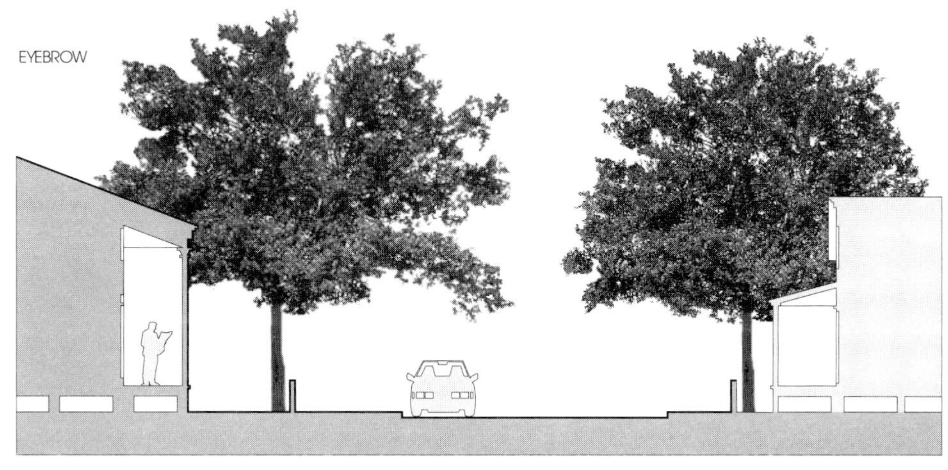
EYEBROW

SAWTOOTH

COMPARATIVE MATRIX

BUILDING TYPE:

CONCH BAHAMA

CONCH FOUR SQUARE

CONCH MANSION

BUILDING TYPE:

CONCH SHOTGUN

CONCH BUNGALOW

CONCH COTTAGE

CONCH SIX-BAY

COMPARATIVE MATRIX

BUILDING TYPE:

CONCH CAPTAIN

CONCH ONE-AND-A-HALF-STORY

CONCH TEMPLE

Building Type:

Conch Eyebrow

Conch Sawtooth

Conch Guest House

Conch Temple

BIBLIOGRAPHY

Caemmerer, Alex. *The Houses of Key West.* Sarasota, Florida: Pineapple Press, 1992.

Linsley, Leslie. *Key West Houses.* New York: Rizzoli, 1992.

"*The Secretary of the Interior's Standards for Rehabilitation and Design Guidelines in Key West's Historic District.*" Historic Architectural Review Commission, City of Key West, Florida, 1991.

Windhorn, Stan and Wright Langley. *Yersterday's Key West.* Key West, Florida: Langley Press, 1990.

McAlester, Virginia and Lee. *A Field Guide to American Houses.* New York: Alfred A. Knopf, 1990.

Nichols, Stephen. *A Chronological History of Key West.* Key West, Florida: Key West Images of the Past, Inc., 1989.

Stresau, Fredric. *Florida, My Eden.* Port Salerno, Florida: Florida Classics Library, 1986.

Cox, Christopher. *Key West Campanion.* New York: St Martin's Press, 1983.

Wells, Sharon and Lawson Little. *Portraits: Wooden Houses of Key West.* Key West, Florida: Historic Key West Preservation Board, 1982.

Starr, Roger. "*The Carpenter-Architects of Key West.*" American Heritage Magazine, Volumne 23, No. 2, February, 1975.

Conch Eyebrow

ABOUT THE AUTHOR

Erick Valle is an assistant professor of the School of Architecture at the University of Miami, in Coral Gables. His interest in urban taxonomy is only superseeded by his knowledge of digital representation. He has a Master of Architecture in Suburb and Town Design, an industrial, urban and architectural design background and his own design practice in the City of Miami.

Conch Eyebrow